phy John Angerson

eorge's Crypt
taining Angels

ST
GEORGE'S
CRYPT

Acknowledgements

Published by St George's Crypt
Great George Street, Leeds LS1 3BR
Telephone: 0113 245 9061
admin@stgeorgescrypt.org.uk   www.stgeorgescrypt.org.uk

Editor Ian Clayton
©Text: St George's Crypt and contributing authors
©Design: Brahm Design
Contemporary photographs: ©John Angerson
The right of John Angerson to be identified as the author
of this photographic work has been asserted by him in accordance
with the Copyright, Designs and Patents Act 1988.

ISBN 0-9534464-1-7
Classification: History/Photography
St George's support team: Martin Patterson, Nicola Goldsmith,
Tim Francis, Judith Hudson, Tina Fields, Katie Sanderson,
John Flounders,Tony Beswick, David Hawkins, Denise Elvy
St George's Crypt is a registered charity No 250016

We acknowledge with grateful thanks the support of the following without whom the production of this book would not have been possible.

The Archbishop of York – for kindly agreeing to write the preface to the book

Barclays – for generous financial support towards the cost of the book

Brian Lewis – for valuable support in interviewing contributors and collating their thoughts

Castles Plc – for generous financial support towards the cost of the paper for the book

Clare Morrow – for contributing the introduction

Cy Chadwick – for interviewing clients, supporters and staff in the initial Action Time Television Programmes promoting the book

Jennie Beaumont and Park Lane College – for great support of the Creative Writing Group

John Angerson – for producing the contemporary photography

Julie Hanson, Lee Bradley and Kate Gledhill from Brahm – for designing the book free of charge and steering the production process

Malcolm Cowing and Catherine Thorpe from Brahm – for coordination and advice on PR for the book

Martyn Duffield and Vicky Chapman at Duffield Printers – for printing the book free of charge

Martin Sheppard – for advice on promotion

Mike Best – for providing the original idea to encourage clients to write their stories

National Institute of Adult Continuing Education (NIACE) – for funding the forerunner of this publication thereby encouraging wider participation in creative writing throughout the charity

Noel Whittall – without whose enthusiasm, commitment and natural rapport with clients this project would never have got off the ground

Peter Cook – for the vision and determination that ensured the project was successfully executed throughout the filming stages with Yorkshire Television and for securing valuable support from many companies who have contributed towards the publication, notably the Yorkshire Television Action Time Charitable Trust

Rosita Whittall – for the painstaking and vital work of proof reading the drafts

Steve Huison – for project work with clients and creative support towards the book

Sylvia Poulson – for faithfully typing up early drafts

Tony Hester – for generous financial support towards the cost of the paper for the book

Yorkshire Post Newspapers for use of Archive Images

All those who contributed in any way either through providing anecdotes or other support to make this book possible

Special thanks to our contributors

Pat Curry	Avril Taylor	Trevor Marsh	David Judge
Jack Curry	Julia Oldfield	John Richards	Matthew Everitt
Mona Wise	Denise Elvy	Archbishop of York	Duncan Johnstone
Brian Blackwell	Pat Stewart	Sidney Fielden	Robert Bloomfield
Pat Trentham	Geraldine Williams	Robin Carmichael	Tony
D Smith	Stephen Williams	Judith Hudson	Gary Stott
Hilda Jean Young	Eileen Atkinson	Martin Patterson	Brian Lewis
Sheila Jowitt	Ian Robins	Alan Armitage	David Hawkins
Jessie King	Gertrude Robins	Matt Armitage	Tim Francis
Jim Sollitt	Geoff Horne	Jack Appleyard	Arnold Ziff
Penny Norman	Malgosia Hurford	Cilbie Appleyard	Jennie Beaumont
Shirley Peacock	Barbara Rainey	Terry Maguire	Jonathan Morgan
Margaret Johnson	Tony Waite	Alex Wright	Des Murphy
John Gainforth	Jim Cairns	Kath Cropper	Ryan
Gladys Benn	Gemma Turner	Donna Cropper	Zico
Darren Williams	Peter Mitchell	Randy Weekes	Steve Brown
Patricia Power	Billy Winrow	Gerry New-Illnahum	Bill Drummond
Craig Lewis	Jimmy Kilpatrick	Neil Walpole	Phillip Clarke
Jack Hinchliff	Harry Smith	Nicholas Clews	John Flounders
Margaret Hinchliff	Freda Matthews	Pam Paterson	Paul Nichols
Edith Daley	Dot Dearnley	Tony Beswick	
Vera Monkby	Peter Mossmann	Margaret McDonaugh	
Mrs Turvick	Honor Mossmann	Mark Tabert	
Eric Johns	Paul Nichols	Derek Marshall	
Margaret Bennett	Jimmy Allen	Patti Lunnis	
Heather Graham	Joe Moss	Simon Coulton	
Betty Throup	Muriel Moss	Sean Rhatigan	

John Angerson

Contents

Foreword

It is a privilege and a pleasure to be able to write a foreword for this fascinating collection of anecdotes about St George's Crypt through the ages.

The Crypt occupies a special place in the hearts of many in Leeds and beyond including those who have travelled from West Yorkshire to many different parts of the world.

The stories you will read in this compilation capture in such a lively and human way the personalities of so many connected with the Crypt, be it as a member of staff, volunteer, supporter, client or friend. The book also gives the reader a vivid snapshot of life in Leeds from 1930 and the many changes which the city has experienced since that time between the two World Wars.

I have known the work of the Crypt for many years, starting during my time in Wakefield and was delighted to be invited to perform the service of rededication for the reopening in 1999. The secret of the Crypt is that those who come through the doors are accepted as they are – the Crypt is an excellent example of the Church being open to and responding to the most basic needs of hundreds of homeless and rootless people who pass through these doors every week.

So many of the stories you will read portray images of remarkable characters – the words on the stained glass window dedicated to the Crypt's former warden, the Reverend Don Paterson, are just so apt: 'You were a Stranger and I took you in'.

The Crypt provides sustenance and warmth to its clients who really depend on the services provided – it is a lifeline to those who feel rejected by society and provides hope to so many whose lives otherwise lack purpose.

I commend *Entertaining Angels* to you –
I do hope you enjoy what you read.

+David Ebor:
Archbishop of York

Introduction

Homelessness is an age old problem. For those who have nowhere to go the situation is no less harsh in the 21st century than it was in the 1930s. For most of society it is something which happens to someone else, something that must have been 'their' fault, something easier to ignore and turn away from than to embrace. *Entertaining Angels* tells the stories of hundreds of people touched by homelessness, and the spirit which shines through their encounters with each other and the rest of the world. What they all have in common is the warmth and friendship offered at St George's Crypt – for some people a lifeline.

The memories are evocative; of times past, but also of situations still happening in the city of Leeds today. From an 81 year old woman who waited for the scraps left from breakfast and hoped for occasional presents of clean clothes, to the man who collected old newspapers from bins and then handed them out like a paper delivery boy for everyone to read.

These are also the stories of the men and women who drink themselves into oblivion, of those whose shoes fit so badly that their toe nails grow underneath their feet, and of the scores of helpers from all walks of life whose care and dedication have helped to make lives a little better.

Collectively their memories and the photographs which go with them capture the history of the Crypt over more than 70 years. We are proud to have been involved in this project.

Clare Morrow, Controller of Programmes, Yorkshire Television

This special place

You could write this story by telling that nearly one hundred years after it was built, St George's Crypt was swept out by volunteers supervised by the Vicar, who then helped serve soup and sermons to the needy. That the Church spire fell down in a gale in the 1960s. That there have been major structural changes made to both Crypt and Church in the 1950s and again in the 1990s. You could tell it like that. But the real story of this special place is in the people who have touched it and who in turn have been touched by it.

The great American folklorist Alan Lomax once said that 'it is the voiceless people of the planet who hold in their memories the generations of human life and wisdom'.

In editing this book I have tried to avoid authorial intervention. All the stories here are told in the first person, just as they were told to me. Some are raw, some sophisticated, there is much beautiful literature too. At the start I set a target. I would talk to 100 people, the one thing they would have in common would be the Crypt. Here then are stories from Archbishops, ex meths drinkers, young people trying to access further education, people who care. I also tracked down the only man still living who walked into the Crypt when the key was first turned back in 1930.

When people look back to the early years of the 21st century they might recall a certain catch phrase. You can hear it every day now, in offices, factories, bars; it involves a tut-tut, toss of the head and a slight wringing of hands and it goes, 'Too much information!! – I didn't need to know that!' People say it when they're embarrassed, when they feel a bit uncomfortable, perhaps when they're trying to be witty or sarcastic after hearing a confessional or personal story.

Over the last couple of decades I have worked on more than 30 books where reminiscence and remembered anecdotes have been at the fore. I have listened to hundreds of elderly members of the community tell me that they had an outside toilet when they were young, that they had bread and dripping for tea nearly every day and that the young people of today wouldn't survive if they had to go through what they put up with.

Ian Clayton
Yorkshire Television

John Angerson

But what do you do when you're confronted by a bright as a button 76 year old lady who tells you that she slept in rainy back streets, or another who talks about the fear of a drunken, brutal husband? How do you listen to a young man who sells *The Big Issue*, who wants to talk about his heroin addiction and the amount of back rent he owes. What about the middle-aged lady who cries as she tells the story of childhood let-downs and the effect it has had? I can't offer trained therapy; I write books and collect stories. Should I wring my hands and say 'Too much information!'?

I have worked collecting stories in top-security prisons, with young offenders on probation, alongside opera singers at the hospital for neurological injury at Putney and on a Tony Harrison film where the dialogue was partly in ancient Greek.

This Crypt project has probably removed more scales from my eyes than all the others put together. There is a lot of information here and we need to know it.

It starts when my former boss at Yorkshire Television, Mike Best, asks if I might like to be involved in doing a story-telling workshop at St George's. Martin Patterson, who heads Publicity and Fundraising there, sets up an afternoon workshop. Attending are a mother and daughter, who have to leave after an hour because they 'have some business to attend to'. One man who sleeps for the entire two-hour session and then wakes up to write a poem about sleeping. Another man who speaks in a jumble of phrases and single-syllable sounds and tells me that he has just seen the 18th century in a dustbin. And finally a young man who arrives half way through the session and demands that I read all of his work before I leave and proceeds to pull out at least a hundred sides of A4 paper hand-written in pencil. *I'm your shadow*, a poem that appears in this book is one of those pieces. A couple of weeks later I read some of that afternoon's work at a breakfast business meeting at Addleshaw Booth Solicitors, to an audience of well-heeled Leeds people. The work of that morning is continued when funders NIACE set up a creative writing group with writer and tutor Noel Whittall, and a small anthology *Crypt Collection 1* is produced. Yorkshire Television become involved again when Regional Features producer Peter Cook decides that the story of St George's Crypt through the eyes of its clients, workers and funders is an ideal project for the 'Action Time' series.

The idea of a community book is of course to affect the community. To allow everyone involved to tell their story. We can't pretend for one minute that the St George's Crypt 'community' is one big happy bunch of people all getting along with each other on a level playing field. A place where part-time staff can engage in conversation with the funders and where the volunteers would go to the theatre with the casual client. What we can do is ensure that people from all the relevant areas of this 'community of shared interest' can tell a tale. From these stories of the Crypt's past, its present and its future, we can work towards a worthwhile process that has an end product. Something like this bonny book you've now got in your hands. Too much information? I don't think so.

Ian Clayton

Don Robins arrives at St George's Church as Vicar in 1930. He surveys the local area and notices the unemployment, the poverty, the lack of educational opportunity and need for nourishment, both spiritual and dietary. Beneath the Church is a Victorian crypt stuffed full of decaying coffins. He decides to clear room in there and set up a soup kitchen which is open to anybody.

During the Second World War he embraces both refugees and German prisoners of war. The Crypt is still a dark, unventilated and foul-smelling place without light, heat or drainage, but is filled with willing and cheery volunteers working long hours without pay. Don himself works tirelessly and dies while still only 48.

Part One of this book includes the voices of those who knew Don Robins personally, with several anecdotes from his son. There are also stories from early Crypt volunteers, workers and clients and the voices of local residents and people who found themselves in the thick of the depression and war years.

Send these, the homeless, tempest-tossed to me.

Emma Lazarus

Part One

You thought his arms were round you

1930 – 1948

Above:
Old Leeds

West Yorkshire Archive Service Leeds

Then there were streets, streets and streets of people, streets full of poor kids, kids that wore wellingtons in the summer time.

Let me paint you the backdrop. Across the road from the Medical School was Nelsons Chemists, a family called Burns lived under the Post Office, there was Hemingways butchers, Hollidays Off-Licence, a little bread shop and even a shop that just sold Spirella corsets. Then there were streets, streets and streets of people, streets full of poor kids, kids that wore wellingtons in the summer time. When you came home from the Gaumont Cinema or Cookridge Street Baths there would be people with big white pots of tea sitting on the doorsteps. Always around and in his robes, I can't remember seeing him in a suit, was Don Robins. Don Robins knew everybody and everybody knew Don. He was truly a part of this community. A lot is said about community these days and a lot of wrong has been committed in the name of 'community'. The community I'm talking about is not an abstract notion, but a real, living thing. Don could remember your name, not because he thought he had to, but because he made a point of wanting to.

☐ What were once distinct memories take on a bit of a dream-like quality with the passing years. I recall confirmation at St George's at 16 and a said Eucharist on the Wednesday evening after. My father going to work, when he had any, without food, so there would be more for the children. I have a picture in mind of men digging trenches for air raid shelters on Woodhouse Moor. Another of Don Robins rolling his sleeves up the minute he walked in the room. I recall Mother being terribly impressed when once she was washing up and Don started to dry the dishes. I vividly see a bench in a corridor in front of a shelf on which sat a typewriter, antique even for those days. I typed Don's letters on it. Then I dished out sandwiches and hauled blankets; I loved being down in the Crypt and doing. And upstairs and outside was all that unemployment, that awful unemployment.

☐ There were no job centres and young bits of lasses asking you 'How many certificates have you got?', 'Are you prepared to work split shifts?'. You did what you could for next to nowt. And if you'd nowt left after pay day you did without. There was a joke at the time. A bloke goes into the butchers and says 'Sell us a sheep's head butcher. And leave the eyes in, it'll see us through the week'.

☐ I had lodgings up Lisbon Street, below where the Yorkshire Post is now. Then I slept in a long room like the army. I worked with a lot of Irish lads. If there was six of us in a potato gang, three would be Irish. It was back-breaking work. You were glad of a swill, good grub and a bed at Shaftesbury House. One of the Irish lads told me that his mates back home had said 'When you get to England, look for Leeds. When you get to Leeds, ask for Shaftesbury House'. It was a Sally Army place. I spent a lot of time between here and there.

☐ Sir Granville Gibson had a tannery up Bramley. You could always get work there because you would go home smelling like nothing on earth and nobody wanted that. I worked there unhairing goat skins from South Africa. I sprayed them. I wore rubber gloves up to my elbow, armlets, an apron and big boots. They had great big drums as high as a room to break all the stiffness out of the skins. When they were finished the skins were as thin as a toilet roll and went for the luxury handbag trade.

☐ I went ditching near Birmingham. Digging long rows down to the clay to drain fields. I thought about the rows of streets near Green Lane school. The streets were that long the numbers went above 70.

☐ We came here from the countryside, Father in search of work. He had been a gardener at the Malham Tarn estate of Captain and Mrs Hutton-Croft. They didn't want him once he became too old. I went from a school with seven pupils to St George's School which had over 300. On the first day the gym mistress told me to jump over the horse. I looked at her and said 'But you haven't got any'. Everybody laughed. At Malham my teacher rode to school on a horse from Middle House Farm. The two winters either side of our move to the city for work linger down the years. In 1936 Mother sat on the landing watching the snow; it snowed and snowed so bad that it came over the wall tops. Our Christmas cake was five miles down the road in Settle and that's where it had to stay.

Top:
Don Robins at the Crypt Sale
1947

Bottom:
Willow Grove Hall,
Serving tea at the Canteen
1946

Next spread:
Soldiers Club
1945

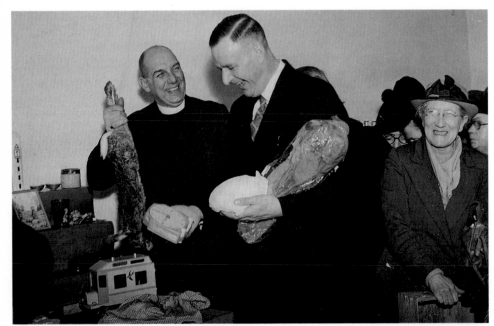

Ten days before Christmas the following winter we sat as a family in the congregation at St George's Church. And a week later we watched the procession of people walk down to the altar carrying decorated trees. We all got a present that year, even Dad got a handkerchief. Don Robins had made a point of welcoming some new people to the area. I believe he was the most marvellous man I have ever met. He had a big smile and a cheery word for all; there was absolutely no side to him. Everything he did and said was kindness itself, you could be royalty or a down-and-out. I retired to Crossgates nearly twenty years ago and I have yet to see a minister.

☐ There was terrific excitement when Don Robins decided to survey the area before he became Vicar at St George's. He decided to do it from the air. He flew over the whole area in a plane. I recall my school friends and I being terribly impressed by a Vicar called Robins who flew.

☐ When Mr Robins spoke his arms would go up and down like an aeroplane. He said that he'd been thinking for a while about wanting volunteers. We were at 59a George Street at the time; I can't have been 14 because I was still at school. The cobwebs had to be got rid of and we cleaned the stones up by getting down on our hands and knees and scrubbing. There was no light. I think they brought electricity down with a cable and we fetched the water in buckets. It only opened at night at first and they let about 16 people in. I used to like watching 'em fight like hell in the queue. Some of the first people to help were firemen's wives. There was a Fire Brigade down Park Street and the women would pool their dripping to make sandwiches and bring over great enamel jugs full of cocoa.

☐ A school was built across the road not long after the Church to give care and education, the key to a better quality of life. Soon afterwards the same motives prompted the building of St Andrew's Church with its own school, in the poorest area between Burley Road and Kirkstall Road.

☐ When Mr Ferriby was the curate, we used to come up in a snake from St George's School every Wednesday afternoon during Lent. They showed us religious films.

☐ St Andrew's was a lovely little school, attached to St Andrew's Church on Cavendish Street. There's not much of that street left now apart from the *Highland Laddie* pub. Back in the 1930s children would be laid to sleep on little grey camp beds in the afternoon. Don Robins would come round to the school with his little dog. It was a Jack Russell or something. He would put a stick against the wall and the dog would jump over it for our amusement. Don was full of charisma. He talked to everybody, it didn't matter whether your Dad was a coalman, like mine, or who he was. Some of my earliest memories are of those little grey camp beds, and of Don Robins' bald head and the visits he made to St Andrew's – they called it the daughter Church of St George's.

☐ Donald Robins was the most marvellous orator; his sermons were wonderful. But beyond that there was something about him that drew everybody to him the minute he walked into a room. I was told that he had been a pilot in the First World War and that a lot of what he saw and did had made him the man he later became. I believe his own enemy was his inability to rest. He was told that he must rest a thrombosis, but when anybody needed him he would go.

☐ He was a big, gorgeous bear of a man. You felt as though his arms were round you even if you were just standing near him. I could cry now when I think about him and I'm thinking about something that happened over 60 years ago. I am five, running near the Medical School. I run straight into Don in his robes. I step back, put my head down and run on a little bit quicker. Don isn't the sort to say 'Mind where you're going'. He just smiles and waves. Later the air-raid siren goes and he comes across to troop us into Church. He gives all of us spoonfuls of condensed milk and we're not afraid. With Don there, nobody is afraid.

A sixpenny bowl of soup at the Harper Street Cafe or a pint of tea and a chinwag at the Crypt meant a lot.

☐ Sometimes during the war we had our services in the school hall. It was at the time of the Battle of the River Plate at Montevideo. Don included a prayer for German soldiers as well. I remember the following day a lot of people being most indignant. They were all discussing it and saying 'Do you know Don Robins has been saying prayers for Germans!'

☐ Today he would be called 'the people's priest'. My father, who had absolutely no time for the established Church, made a special case for Don Robins. His particular brand of humanitarian Christianity struck a chord with Christians and agnostics alike. We were all working class kids who lived in what is now the inner city; to us it was home. The highlight of St George's Cub year was the summer camp Mr Robins organised to Appletreewick. Many of the boys' dads were serving abroad, one friend's dad was in a Japanese POW camp. Every morning we were marched down to a river where Don, up to his knees in water, would pour buckets full of icy cold river over our heads. We marched back to camp sniffing the aroma of the day's porridge as it simmered in pots over an open fire. We would climb to the top of Simon's Seat one day, and on another visit Trollers Ghyll. Our leader Don was like the kind of uncle not many of us had and we were like pit ponies on a day off!

☐ My Father was an ecclesiastical, geometrical, blue metal twister for William Pape of Queen Street. As such he did all the window repairs at St George's until he was called up for the Second World War. Many a time he told me that whenever he was called upon to work there, Don Robins would find time to talk to him about his family, his work and offer cups of tea.

Now, for as long as I can remember, on the nearest Sunday to Armistice Day there was a big parade of all territorial and reserve regiments in the Leeds area. They paraded around the City Centre with their bands and finished up with a big church service at St George's. After the service Don Robins would always make a point of going down the lines of men and to the amazement of many of the soldiers he stopped and had a word with my Dad and addressed him by name.

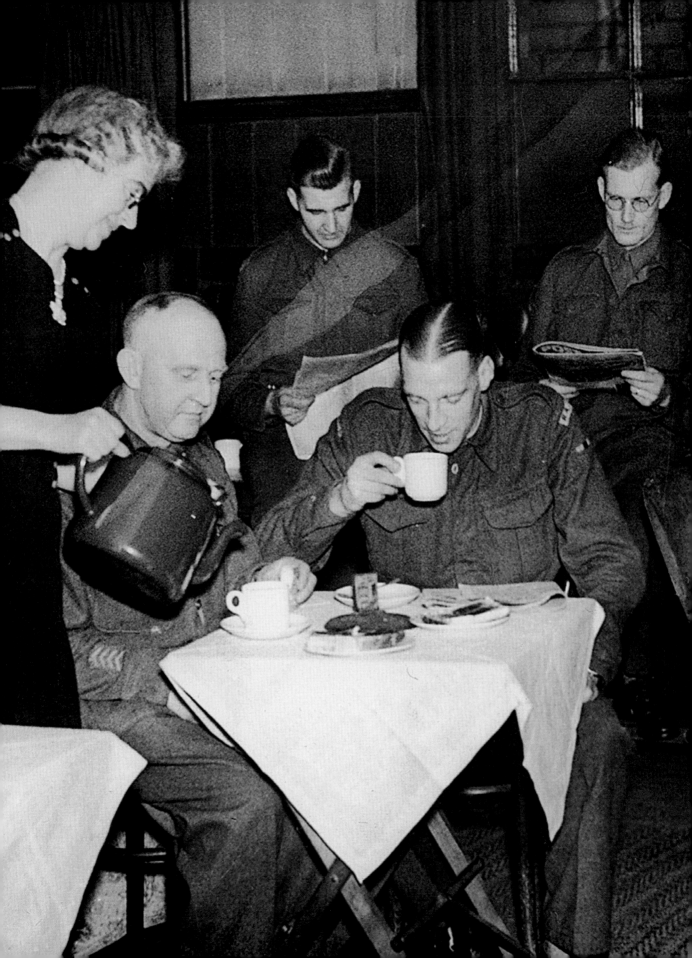

In my child's mind I told myself
that it would go to somebody more
deserving than me, but all these
years later, whenever I hear anybody
mention the Christmas Tree Service,
I'm still left wanting that doll.

Crypt archive

Crypt archive

Top left:
German prisoners of war

Top right:
Afternoon tea
1950

☐ I was a paper boy on Tonbridge Street. The German prisoners were based up at Butcher's Hill. The army brought them down to Fenton Street Barracks to sort out clothes from the battlefields. I was in the Newsagents on Willow Terrace Road. Some German soldiers came in. I was in absolute awe. I'd heard all about German soldiers and there were some standing right next to me in uniform with metal helmets on, I think they had cloth diamonds sewn on their backs. One of them talked to me in good English and asked me where he might go to worship. I told him that there was a Vicar at St George's who welcomed German prisoners. Otto later became my friend. He gave me a photo of himself in the Afrika Korps. I carried it about for years, but sadly I've lost it now.

☐ They had a little Mission Hall down Bramah Street to try and encourage people to come to church. What a lot won't realise these days is that the church played a major part in our lives. Not just the Christian worship, but the social side of it as well. On Easter Mondays we'd go for hikes up to Fewston Reservoir and Blubberhouses. We had regular whist drives and dances; it was what they called 'Home Efforts'. Our group was called 'The Five Fairies', Freda and Beatrice Clark were twins, there was Minnie Beaumont, Peggy Smith and me. Bob Stone had a band and they played Henry Hall and Harry Roy stuff. We organised dances for him. Healeys Confectioners on Little Woodhouse Street did all their own baking and provided buns and stuff. On Bonfire night we had fish and chips provided by Youngmans and packets of sparklers and we'd all do the sparkler dance. At Christmas time the church was full to bursting and we'd all decorate the trees with sugar mice and bird cages from a shop on Park Lane called Granelli's.

☐ Mr Robins wanted to hold a Nativity play in the Crypt. I was a cabinet maker, so I ended up building a stage and then making an infant's cot. To top it off I was asked to play Joseph!

☐ People brought tea, sugar, margarine. Even an aspidistra plant from my Mother's house in Portland Crescent ended up in what they called 'The Palm Court'.

The benches they used came from the Memorial Chapel, a side chapel in the church. These had been replaced by chairs with name plaques on them dedicated to men who didn't come back from the First War.

☐ My Dad decorated bakelite beakers to raise funds. Woolworths had this line in plain bakelite beakers; my Dad cleared them out of them. He copied scenes from nursery rhyme books and Snow White.

☐ It was one of the year's most exciting outings – to be allowed to join the Scouts riding on an open truck, going out to Bolton Abbey in Wharfedale. Our consignment – a pile of Christmas trees, most of them about four feet high, but also two great twenty foot trees, to be decorated and set each side of the Sanctuary at St George's for the annual Christmas Tree Service. The smaller trees – some 100 of them – would be mounted by the Scouts, and set in rows in the school hall, each tree carefully labelled, for example 'Husband, wife, boy aged 2, girl aged 5, girl aged 6'. The trees were allocated to organisations or individuals within the church family, who would then be responsible for decorating a number of trees, adding gifts suitable for the age of each child in the family to which they would be sent.

These trees were then carried in procession for dedication at the annual Christmas Tree Service, to which the congregation brought their gifts of new and second-hand toys for the free Christmas Toy Shop. This shop was open to around 500 registered families, and parents were invited to choose a new and a second-hand toy for each of their children, taking them home *as their own gifts to their children.*

Just before Christmas Day, cars would appear, lent by willing drivers, and transporting scarlet robed Father Christmases, taking the Christmas trees out to the homes for which they had been lovingly prepared. I remember one year when we were short of a Father Christmas. Though really too young, nevertheless I was crammed into a Father Christmas outfit, and sent out to the slums of St Andrew's Parish. I shall never forget scrambling down the winding stone staircase of a basement hovel, to find partially dressed children staring in disbelief and excitement as I gave them their Christmas surprise.

Someone Cares

Crypt archive

Above:
Crypt Appeal Brochure
1946

Top left:
Scenes at the Christmas Toy Distribution
1947

Far right:
'I think I'll have this one'
1947

☐ My Aunty Nelly's aunt had a porcelain doll. I wanted that doll. Just before Christmas one year I was handed the doll and told to take it down to the Crypt as a gift for the Christmas Tree Service. Someone would receive it as their Christmas present. I have never wanted anything as much as that doll. I daren't ask for it. You know how it is when you know that you're not supposed to ask for things. I wanted to say 'I'll give you all my things if I can just have that doll'. All through the Christmas Tree Service I looked at the doll and made plans in my mind to get it. In my child's mind I told myself that it would go to somebody more deserving than me, but all these years later whenever I hear anybody mention the Christmas Tree Service, I'm still left wanting that doll.

☐ Sometimes you don't know how poor you are until somebody tells you. I knew a lot of the people who got stuff given because I lived against them. I often came home to tell my Mother that 'so and so had been given some biscuits and cocoa'. I can't remember us being given so much as a ha'penny or cup of tea. It's like a three star hotel now, they're better off than I am.

☐ We had a little fish shop at the bottom of West Street near Grace Street. There were some people who you couldn't bear to take money off. My Dad often gave away a twopenny fish and a penn'orth.

☐ The smell of Izal disinfectant carries me back instantly to the early days of the Crypt. Men who had been walking from town to town in search of work, rarely having the opportunity to wash, and sleeping in whatever accommodation they could find, often lying together for warmth under railway arches – such men were often ridden with vermin.

Crypt archive

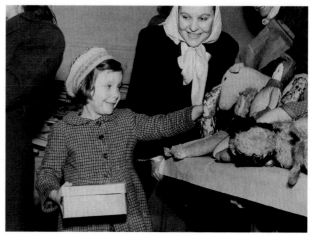

Crypt archive

At all costs the Crypt had to maintain a standard of cleanliness, and this was achieved by mop-washing throughout the public areas at least twice a day. The atmosphere of disinfectant struck you forcibly as you entered the main door, and clients and the scores of volunteer workers lived and breathed that pungent pong day in, day out.

☐ Certain figures stand out in my memory of boyhood days around the Crypt – Tommy Facer, Verger and general factotum, always on hand for odd jobs around the Crypt and the church; properly robed on Sundays to welcome the congregation, issuing books, controlling lighting and dealing with emergencies. Austin Walker, Caretaker for the schools, driver of the Crypt van, strong pair of hands when any heavy work was required. Mollie Brooks, elderly senior citizen, on duty most mornings behind the Crypt counter, making sandwiches, brewing tea and bantering with the men as they came in for their mid-morning snack. Numerous office workers – Joan, Peggy, Doris, Kitty, Judith – my memory fails me – but many more were there, some paid staff working longer hours than ever they were paid for, many volunteers, coming straight from work in typing pools in the City, eating a sandwich and settling down to work for the evening on the massive typewriters of those days. I don't remember anyone complaining of repetitive strain syndrome, though surely their fingers must have been worn down by home time!

☐ He was a regular customer for morning tea, registered blind, and always tap-tapping his way along the pavement. On this particular sunny morning the entrance to the Crypt was jammed with the parked prams of the Young Mums' Group. He steered his way faultlessly between the gridlocked push-chairs, shaded his eyes to check the time high on the church tower clock, and then continued tapping his way to the Crypt Rest Room!

☐ I was born on a stone kitchen floor 81 years ago and I've slept in fields and in dustbins many a time. When you're a frightened young woman with nowhere to go and you daren't go home, you're thankful for small mercies. A sixpenny bowl of soup at the Harper Street Cafe or a pint of tea and a chin-wag at the Crypt meant a lot. I courted a chap who got the old fellers their breakfast at the Crypt and when he'd done he would save me some and just now and again he'd fetch me some clean clothes.

He took me by the hand and said 'I'm going to take you somewhere now, because I want to show you something that will make you realise how lucky you are.'

If it was a cold day and Don saw somebody shivering without a top coat on, he would take off his own and give it to them.

☐   Just before 'lights out' my father, a Curate, or another member of staff would join the men and invite any who wished to come for evening prayers in the tiny Crypt Chapel. Twenty or so would shuffle through, and I would grind the harmonium into action so that they could sing a chosen hymn – usually it was 'Abide with me' – 'Hold thou thy cross before my closing eyes...' and I can never forget the tragedy of those workless and broken men contrasting with the comfort to which I would shortly return, as the night watchman locked the Crypt gates, and my father and I drove home to the Vicarage.

☐   It was at a Thursday evening meeting that Don Robins told us about his idea of having a look inside the Crypt. I'm the only person alive now who was there when he fetched the key and turned it in the lock of the iron gate. Mr Robins led the way followed by me, Jim Taylor and another young fellow whose name I can't bring to mind now. His torch shone on the walls as we walked on four inches of dust like a thick rich carpet. Some of the panels had dropped off the coffins with age and we could see women's hair hanging down two or three feet long. Even walking by walls where people had been laid years before gave you an eerie feeling. The lads thought it would be an impossible task to do anything with the place, but the girls thought otherwise; they had far more faith and put their hands up to volunteer.

☐   I can go back before Don Robins' time to Mr Herklots and Mr Adams. Don came up from Croydon. He told us that he was flying over the English Channel when he was told to come into the ministry. He was an angel. My Auntie Lily and Auntie Norah went to the Thursday evening Young People's Fellowship. Don didn't say what he wanted them to do, but he asked for volunteers to turn up on the Saturday. They arrived dressed up, like people did on a weekend at that time. Don had opened up the Crypt and had wheelbarrows and shovels waiting, the whole place was ankle deep in dust. Lily and Norah went home as black as a pair of crickets. My Granny was mad. They were ever so pleased to do their bit.

☐ At Leeds Salem Chapel, towards the end of his life, Don told of an experience in the Royal Flying Corps. Apparently, one night he had a bitter quarrel with another officer and both retired to bed without reconciliation. The other officer was on dawn patrol next morning and was shot down and killed. His body was recovered and given a military funeral. Don was hurt that he was not asked to be a pall-bearer. When he queried this, a colleague said 'We didn't think you were friends'. On that day Don vowed that never again would he let the sun go down on a quarrel. He said that it was the first step along the path which led to his becoming Vicar of St George's and to the founding of the Crypt.

☐ Don started to work himself into the ground before he died. February 3rd was a bitterly cold day for a funeral. We sang:

The king of love my shepherd is,
Whose goodness faileth never;
I nothing lack if I am His
And He is mine forever.

Everybody cried in lumps and the tears came like ice onto our cheeks.

☐ Thousands came. Two bishops, forty odd clergymen, members of the Jewish community, the Council, Police and a lot that the Police might have moved on any other day. One tramp walked over from Rochdale. Another tramped all the way from Birmingham.

☐ I have an image in my mind I will always retain. I'm in my Granny's basement kitchen at Portland Crescent. I am sitting on Don Robins' knee. He has made me the Lord Mayor's chain out of safety pins and jam-jar lids.

Crypt archive

They'd say 'Well you've got a lovely husband, a nice home, two beautiful children, why do you want to be among those horrible men?'

Reportage Photography
John Angerson

Poetry workshop

On this page is Steve Brown's poem "I'm your shadow". On pages 90 and 91 are further poems from the workshop, Sleep by Terry Maguire and an untitled work by Alex Wright.

I'm Your Shadow
I creep around late at night
Always within people's sight
I dance around without a sound
Gripping every corner of the
pavement and walls
But most of all
I'm your shadow.

I enter your house without a sound
And watch you creep around.
You treat me like a prisoner
When you don't go out
But I'm always there
Without a doubt
Sometimes you treat me like a fool
But don't forget I was there
When you went to school
Who am I, I'm your shadow.

I'm just there when you're sitting
On a chair
Or when you're outside
Among the shadows of the street,
Moving and listening
To the sound of clattering feet
Slowly creeping down the street.
I'm your shadow.

As I walk down the street
With you
I meet many other shadows
Some black, some blue
Some dressed in different clothes
And some like you.
If you're walking or running a race
I'm just floating in empty space.
Floating, floating, hugging the ground.
Moving past every obstacle
Without a sound.
I'm part of you as much
As you are of me.
Who am I, look down
And see
I'm your shadow, that's who I be.

The new Vicar Tony Waite arrives and immediately realises that something must be done to continue the good work. He sets up a committee to oversee the day-to-day business of running the soup kitchen and night shelter, now catering for many rough sleepers and homeless men. The war has left many emotionally scarred and alcoholism becomes a major issue as well as the increasing numbers of homeless and workless. Faith Lodge is acquired in a bid to 'move on' and give shelter to people using the Crypt.

A radio broadcast by Wilfred Pickles raises awareness of the Crypt's work, and funds raised following the broadcast allow the Crypt to expand in size and scope. In the 60s women are admitted for the first time. A Medical Centre and a Family Centre are pioneered. Richard Allen, a scholarly graduate from a privileged background turns his back on worldly ambition to become Warden; he is followed by Don Paterson, his protégé. Don works seven days a week until at least 10.00 each night. Don could never give less than his all to the work of the Crypt and he dies while still young, in May 1990.

Part Two includes a rich diversity of voices; Tony Waite himself tells of his first hand experiences, there are tales from doctors, nurses, volunteer workers and more from clients who used the Crypt during this period.

The poor have to labour in the face of the majestic equality of the law, which forbids the rich, as well as the poor to sleep under bridges, beg in the streets and steal bread.

Anatole France

Part Two
By the Grace of God and Wilfred Pickles
1948–1990

I suppose we counselled the men who came here, except they didn't call it counselling then, they called it talking.

Crypt archive

Above:
Crypt contestant
1948

When the war ended, we all thought that it would be the end of suffering. A finish to brutality, torture and cruelty. No more broken homes and families, no more mixed up people. The reality in Leeds was that the slums were slow to fall, Armley Jail was still overcrowded and the schools still churned out fodder for the factories.

☐ There was no Health Service, of course, and no such thing as social welfare. When the State came along in 1948 it was going to embrace all of our problems. All the doss houses would be closed down and the tramps, the unwashed and the down-and-outs would be offered beds on casual wards. It didn't work like that. For six weeks after the NHS was born, St George's Crypt was nearly empty. Then they all came back again. The State couldn't cope.

☐ You might call it a rag, tag and bobtail outfit, a happy-go-lucky, hit and miss set up. Terrible amateurs dabbling in the things we didn't truly understand. We had very few allies. The newspapers looked down on us, the social care professionals were not keen, and even the Salvation Army saw us as competition, though I do recall the Chief of Police being an enormous help. Of course, we were keeping a lot of people off the streets. We had no concept of the psychological needs of our clients and the hygiene standards here did leave a lot to be desired. It was so unbelievably primitive, even to the stage where we would carry dirty washing-up water in buckets out on to the street and empty the contents into drains in the road. I might be prosecuted these days, but I'm sure nobody died as a result of our adventures.

☐ I came from a Parish in Blackheath. When I saw the set up, I knew that I couldn't take on the work Don Robins had been doing. There was no committee, so I helped to start one. Even so, it required a great deal of faith to carry on. By the grace of God and Wilfred Pickles we were able to continue. He came here to see what was going on and decided to record his show 'Have a Go'. The episode went out two nights later and we sat all agog in the Crypt listening to the wireless.

A day later we had a call from somewhere in the north-east and another from London, 'What can we do to help?' A couple of days later Ernest phoned me from Leeds City railway station. 'You'd better come quick Vicar, they can't get any more parcels in t'office'. People who had listened to the show had sent parcels of clothes and food from all parts of the country. Railway van loads continued to arrive over the following days, until a warehouse was commandeered at the station to store it all. Also, £4,000 came in, which was a huge amount of money in those days. This enabled us to improve hygiene standards by constructing a proper kitchen with drainage, and for the first time, ventilation. I heard that when they saw the reaction, the BBC accused Wilfred Pickles of making an appeal. I know he didn't. As he signed off he said 'Well, there's St George's, remember them in your prayers. Good night and God bless'. That's not an appeal.

☐ Some people say 'Ooh! These people!'. If only they knew the stories. Don Paterson knew them and he knew how to put a persuasive and gentle arm around them. I came to know them; it was a culture shock at first. In London I worshipped at St Mary's Islington and nursed small children. When I arrived in Leeds I worked on Ward 9, the Medical Ward, and volunteered here on Wednesday nights. There were men here who had spent a lot of time in mental institutions who didn't know they were ill. There were many who drank *jake*, a mixture of cider and surgical spirit which looked like milk. There were more still who had been ravaged by two world wars. One man told me he could not only still see the bodies, he could smell them. Another man, who came from a well-to-do family in Roundhay had been a pilot; he quoted Psalms and was a brilliant pianist.

Barnsley Bob said to a Neuro
Surgeon 'Before my operation
I used to shout, scream, swear
and cry ... I don't cry now'.

Crypt archive

Above:
Behind the service hatch
1952

☐   Jan was a Polish man who was always very drunk and he had a terrible cough. He came on to my ward when I still worked at the Infirmary. We discovered he had 'open' TB, and he was moved to the sanatorium at Gateforth. Because he was homeless they kept him on after his discharge as an orderly. In the meanwhile Don and I got married and settled in to Faith Lodge. Not long after we had our first child we had a surprise visit from Jan. He came up to Faith Lodge and said 'I have an hour and a half before my bus goes, can I stay for a cup of tea?' He sat drinking his tea and noticed the pram. I proudly showed him the new baby. He looked into the pram and muttered his apologies that he had to go. Much later Don saw Jan when he was visiting the clinic. He said 'I'm sorry I left quickly the last time – but I had a wife and child once'.

☐   Barnsley Bob was a likeable old rogue who had a big beard and had to be kept under a bit of control. Then there was another man who went round the bins in the streets collecting papers. He would come back to the Crypt and give out the newspapers, but always miss me out. I felt a bit snubbed really, as though he was making it an *us and them*. I'm not saying that I wanted a newspaper out of a bin, but it would have been nice to be asked. Then one day he came past me and said 'Would you like a paper?' I knew from that moment that I had been accepted. Years after I'd finished volunteering at the Crypt, I would still get men coming up to me in the street for a chat. I might be out shopping in the town with my husband, and one of the Crypt men would shout. My husband would go on in front and turn round to tell me to 'come on', but I would be wanting to know how they were or if they'd got a house yet.

☐   They got it about that Barnsley Bob had died seven or eight times before he did. He was like Lazarus coming back. At one time he had been a famous coal miner who had an accident. They put a plate in his head. He got good 'compo', and when he had money he was surrounded by tappers. As soon as he twigged what they were doing to him he'd go up in the air. He would take his shoes off and throw 'em across the road from Lewis's, and then hit his steel plate with his hand. He wore the same coat for donkey's years; it was the thickest coat I've ever seen and he wouldn't take it off.

☐ Barnsley Bob had a big operation scar on his head. One day a neuro-surgeon friend of mine came and Bob said to him 'Before I had my operation I used to shout, swear, scream and cry... since my operation I don't cry any more!' We used to say he was like the Town Hall; even if you got him clean, the top of him stayed dirty.

☐ Joe Beck was a big big man, a classic loner, who died the same day as my mother. I could spend most of the night bathing and cleaning his terrible ulcerated legs. He consistently refused to sleep in a bed; we always had to put the mattress down on the floor.

☐ There was one called *Midnight*. If you spoke to him during the night he'd say 'Hello' to you; if you tried to talk to him in the daytime he'd tell you to 'piss off'. Then there was another who'd put his arms around you all friendly like and tell you a soft story. 'I'm sorry I don't know you. Oh! I am sorry I have met you before. I do know your face, but I can't put a name to you. Oh! do excuse me'. And all the time he'd be in your pockets. Very quick indeed. What they call a finger man.

☐ I had not been employed by the Crypt for more than a couple of weeks when I had the privilege of meeting one of the well known characters from the past. He had been a frequent visitor in former years – now he 'looked in' occasionally when he was passing.

I had answered his knock on the door. He came into the foyer area and whilst he had probably had a pint or two he was not the worse for wear. He was friendly and courteous and not having met me before immediately enquired as to who I was. He did not want anything but had 'just called in to see us'. He then began to wax eloquently about the many times he had been helped here at the Crypt. He spoke particularly with great affection and warmth about the late Don Paterson and how wonderful Don had been in helping him on so many occasions.

We spent about five minutes or so just chatting generally when he announced he would be off on his way. He then informed me that usually Don would have given him a parting hug and kiss! He asked me without hesitation 'would you'. I responded with some further light hearted banter as we made our way to the door. However, he was insistent – as he was going through the door, I was shaking his hand when in an instant he gave me a hug and planted a kiss on my cheek! With a huge grin on his face he waved goodbye.

I smiled to myself and thought – yeah, the Beatles were right – after all they were merely repeating the teaching of Jesus when they sang 'All you need is love'.

☐ The people, mostly men, who end up on the streets and go to the Crypt are usually pleasant company. A difficulty they often have is to believe this themselves. It may take weeks, months or years of contact with Crypt staff before this fact emerges.

J and A used to stay at Regent Terrace, the 'wet' house for problem drinkers. Neither of them could stay off the booze for more than a few days, but both responded to the kindness shown to them by becoming kind themselves.

J developed a habit of greeting people with a big bear hug. He was tall – about six-foot-three – and strong. When he saw you in Leeds he would inflict his well-intended but horrible embrace on you. If, like me, you are short you found your face crushed into his rather smelly old coat. When he released you the alcohol on his breath nearly felled you, but it was easy to forgive him because of the genuinely friendly, if wonky, smile through which the fumes emanated.

A was a small and quiet man – almost shy, even when drunk. His pleasantness was a lot less extrovert than that of J. He had a way of talking to you that made you feel good. He never expressed gratitude for anything in particular, but you were made to feel that somewhere in a distant corner of his inebriated memory he recalled something for which he was grateful, and he was therefore glad to see you. Although his conversation was confined to a few simple phrases like 'Hello Doc' or 'How are you?', or 'I'm afraid I'm drunk', he always made his words sound as though they came from the heart.

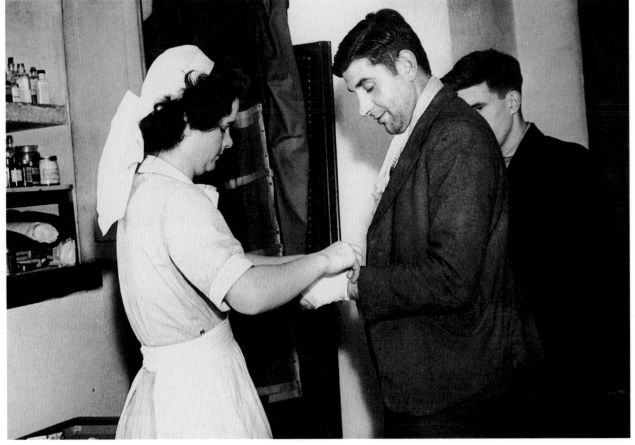

Above:
Treatment for hand wound
1948

☐ Crypt clients were some of the first people I knew who could cope with decimalisation. They were used to little coins in their hands. When I was wondering 'Is that two bob or half a crown?', they knew exactly.

☐ Let's call him Sam. I met him in the late 1960s, the days of flower-power, hippies and hope. The meeting took place in a workhouse-styled bathroom of Middlewood Hospital in Sheffield, where I'd been instructed to clean up our latest admission. I was a psychiatric nurse; he presented as a huge ball of hair from which a voice issued at fifteen-second intervals.

I hoped he would bathe himself. I watched hot, clean water cloud as it lapped against what seemed years of ingrained mud. It was soon obvious that Sam lacked all interest in cleanliness. His single action was to shout 'bollocks' into the distant left-hand corner of the echoing bathroom. I rolled up my sleeves and bent to wash him. I used the opportunity to question him. 'What's the trouble Sam? Who is it you're shouting at?'. No matter how often it happened I was always surprised when people hallucinating, and who you thought to be in the grip of disorientation, began to answer questions in an almost rational manner. 'It's them tormenting again'. 'Who's them?'. 'Them? It's them isn't it? Them that's been following me about, them that drove me from t'Crypt, them that's been pinching me drink'. He became a different man. Alert eyes gleamed up at me from the depths of a hirsute face. He told me about drinking meths, of creatures attacking him for his precious bottle, of fighting in a river, of almost drowning as he clung to his life-enhancing drink. At the end he lapsed again into faraway silence; silence except for the regular aiming of 'bollocks' into that left-hand corner.

As one born and bred in Sheffield my knowledge of Leeds in those days was confined to Elland Road, Headingley Cricket Ground, the Canadian Emigration Office at Leeds station and Queenie's Castle. But I was also aware of St George's Crypt. Over a few years I met several individuals who passed through that place of refuge and support. Some had drink problems, others had mental health problems.

Sam, once clean and shaved of his excess hair, was revealed as a man in his mid-50s with the look of a ravaged 70-year-old. He was officially diagnosed as schizophrenic and alcoholic. Having spent many periods of his life on the tramp he had seen the inside of several northern mental hospitals.

All this we discovered from Sam himself, who became loquacious when stabilised. We also had the advantage of viewing the records held by Sam's previous hospitals. Yet we never discovered where he came from or where he was born. If Sam knew, and I'm sure he did, for whatever reason he was not letting on.

The only constant stable point in Sam's life seemed to be St George's Crypt. Time after time during the horrors of his past that place appeared as the one true asylum, the one place he could rest and experience a relative security – until 'they' drove him away.

Sam left us after four weeks, his destination the Salvation Army Hostel. He left us clean, shaven, with fresh clothing and a week's supply of medication. Everyone knew his stay there would be short, that his medication would soon run out without being replaced and that the chances of him taking it would be slim. Soon he would be back on the road.

He appeared, then disappeared. I've no idea where he went or what happened to him. I can only hope he found his way back to St George's Crypt and this time managed to hang on.

☐   Down-and-outs do not immediately excite our sympathy; rather we think of them as anti-social alcoholics who have finally arrived on skid row. Some are like that; others are portrayed as fiercely independent 'characters' avoiding any attempt by 'do-gooders' to impose some kind of conformity or respectability on them. Some are like that too. But most are not like either of these two caricatures.

Thirty years ago, long after nurses had pricked their consciences, doctors began a regular surgery here. I have been one of a group of doctors trying to meet some of the medical needs of a group of people who are literally the outcasts of society.

As always happens with voluntary work, participation is a revelation. You realise that although the men, and it is mostly men, have much in common with each other, they are very different. The stereotype group identity begins to separate out in Joe, the low-IQ man with epilepsy and no family; Jimmy the kindly alcoholic, who has no more aggression in him than the average goldfish; Pat, the one with schizophrenia whose inability to cope with anybody pushes him back on the streets. Then there is Andy, the illiterate and difficult psychopath, whose explosive temper keeps him from leading any kind of conventional life. There are occasional frightening men, who by clever or bullying tactics hope to obtain drugs. There are inadequate personalities of all sorts, with sad histories behind their dishevelled beards; pathetic men, tired and confused; simple men, but so complicated that no-one can help them. There are a few rogues, a few scroungers, some malingerers, but almost all, through no fault of their own, have ended up homeless and adrift.

I am no saint. After a long or difficult surgery at the end of a working day I have often almost decided to quit as a medical helper. I find that I seldom know how to begin solving these men's fundamental problems, nor do I know how society should provide and care for them. Certainly, I know fewer answers now than when I started. I no longer believe that more than the odd middle-class notion has any relevance to a group at the very bottom of the social pecking order.

Yet I do come back here. I come back because many of the problems here are those which any general practitioner is dealing with daily. We are on the look-out for tuberculosis, gastrointestinal disorders, epilepsy, angina or skin diseases. They may ask for reassurances that aches and pains are no more than that. We listen to tales, real, fanciful or hallucinatory; we help men withdrawing from alcohol. I come back because many of the men are genuinely likeable. I come back because, selfishly, there is emotional satisfaction – even prestige – in being a helper to people so unfortunate. I come back because just now and then I have been able to offer comfort to an ill or suffering individual. I come back because without a hint of false humility I can say that there is not much difference between them and me. We are human, but I have the privileges. I possess a good education, a fulfilling job, a happy family, a faith that inspires me. All these have been given to me. If they had not, perhaps I too would be of no fixed abode, a misfit in a world where officials and charities offer crumbs of comfort, where drink takes some of the hardness out of floors in derelict buildings and the company of other vagrants offers some kind of comradeship and sense of community. Most long-term psychiatric units have closed their doors. We need 'do-gooders' now more than ever.

☐   Austin Walker was a lovely man and his wife was a proper lady. He was the caretaker here and at the school. When I left school I delivered household coal. Austin lived up the Claremonts and I was always invited in for a pot of tea and a sandwich. Before then when I was still at St George's I often stopped behind to help him with the fires and sweep up. He gave me a Rolex watch, and I wore it all the way through school. One day when I was a man, I was shovelling coal and it fell off my wrist. The glass broke and one of the hands came off. I chucked it down a grate in temper. I've regretted doing that a lot of times since. One because it was a silver case and second because it was a gift from Austin Walker. I'll always remember him going round the houses on behalf of the Crypt, dressed up as Santa.

Left:
Men coming in at the gate
1950

Crypt archive

☐ Uncle Tom lived up Stratton Street and drove the little Crypt van. I went with him sometimes when he went to see them with a bit of brass up Lawnswood and Headingley collecting toys and clothes. When Wilfred Pickles came to the Crypt to do *'Have a Go'*, Tom was on the show. There was a part of the show where Wilfred would ask 'If you weren't you, who would you like to be?', Tom replied he would like to be W.D. or H.O.Wills – he loved Woodbines! Once when asked his religion, he replied 'Plymouth Tobacconist'.

☐ Tom Johns had been married before. He was a Catholic at first and then he became C of E. Don was kind to him and offered to marry him in this Church. That might have been when he started to drive the van. When I was young and just learning to drive, the van was garaged up Springfield Mount. He used to chuck me the keys and say 'Go and open the garage and get the van warmed up'. I loved going round with him collecting and delivering at Christmas time. We went to addresses all over, round the bottom of Scott Hall Road and Sheepscar taking biscuits, bars of chocolate and tinned stuff. I worked on the clothing with him as well, next to a big bin full of disinfectant.
   Tom had a fantastic sense of humour. I've seen him in a pub put the flight end of a dart into his ear and then walk round asking people if they've seen anybody throwing darts about. He was once on the television on a programme called *'State your Case'*. Marjorie Proops was one of the judges. You were allowed so much time to say what you would do if you were given £100. If your case was strong enough you got the money. People would say things like 'I'd take my Grandmother on a holiday'. When they asked Tom he astounded everybody by saying 'I'd give the money to my boss'. He then went on to talk about his work at the Crypt and won the prize.

☐ I must confess I dreaded going down to the Crypt amongst the men. Our neighbour Mrs Parker would send me on errands. She was a member of the ladies' fellowship and she would come to our door with her prayer book and say 'Pat, will you go and collect some Church magazines for me'. The magazines were kept on a table downstairs so I had to walk past them all laid out on the pews. Bless them, they would say 'Hello', but they didn't half scare me. I envied our neighbour Mrs Parker. Whatever she got out of the Church, I wanted it.

☐ Brian was an ex Sergeant-Major who came here as a down-and-out. He was converted through Richard Allen. He started off doing a bit of sweeping up and tidying three nights a week. Then he took on the caretaker's job and eventually became an assistant Verger in the Church. He made his bed in a little room here.

☐ Captain Kierle of the Church Army was one of the wardens. He lodged with my sister Margaret and was a lovely, loving Christian man. I took him to meetings on my motorbike and sidecar, because it wasn't always easy to get a bus. He finished up moving down to Cheltenham and twice walked from Lands End to John O'Groats for charity.

☐ I had Crypt clothes which I would sling into the wash often, because of the smoke. To relieve the dreariness of it all there would be plenty of bantering, practical jokes and horse play amongst the hard work. We might all pile back to Theology students' rooms for coffee. And there were plenty of almost surreal moments. Opera North rehearsed in rooms nearby. Among all the chaos you might get Lord Harewood ringing up about something or other. When we painted we wore old pyjamas. Once one of the helpers went out for fish and chips in her pyjamas and was almost guided 'back to the hospital'!

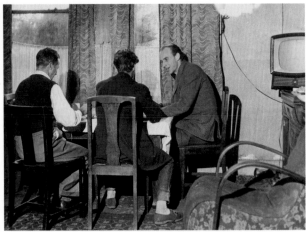

Crypt archive

Above:
Don Paterson talking to men
at Faith Lodge
1970's

☐   Some people have a wide vision on life, others have narrowed their vision down to become very focused. Don Paterson was one of the latter. He was completely sure that the Crypt was God's work and everybody else ought to be doing it as well. I knew this before we were married; I knew he had a vocation and in those days I was more prepared to accept things rather than to fight them. So I knew his work had to come first.

We married and moved in to Faith Lodge with the men. We had one room, a kitchen and a bathroom and upstairs in a large room divided into cubicles were the men. Most were alcoholics and the pretty grim noises they made easily travelled downwards. In three years, bringing up two small children we had just three nights unbroken sleep. Because as well as the men we looked after, we had a 24-hour phone link to answer. There was no Alcoholics Anonymous in Leeds then, and people would phone in the middle of the night from an area that covered Bradford to Hull. It was the same with desperate people, there was no Samaritans either, so concerned telephone operators would often phone us. 'I don't think he's suicidal but I think he needs to talk to somebody'.

☐   Don would spend the first part of his working day up at Faith Lodge watching television with the men and just talking through their problems. For some the story was just so far back in the haze they couldn't be bothered to even find it to tell it. In the early years of our work at Faith Lodge nearly every alcoholic was an alcoholic because of the war. My favourite was Percy. He was totally alcoholic and gorgeous. He proposed to me every night. Don used to say that he finally proposed marriage to stop me saying 'Yes' to Percy!

Every Sunday you might find people in Church in their Sunday clothes in one set of pews, and up to a dozen down-and-outs who smelled awful sitting in another area. It worked both ways. Don liked to keep his men under his wing and some worshippers didn't have to sit next to the smell. At one service Percy pulled a bottle out from under a pew and waved it. I tried to calm him. He looked round and said 'Hello darling, will you marry me?'.

How can anybody go to Church on Sunday and not see the implications of that throughout the week?

Crypt archive

☐ I learned all about sweat, hard work and true comradeship during my time working down the pit at Middleton Broom. Years later I learned how cruel humans can be to their own when I re-trained as a technician at the Home Office mortuary in Leeds.

It is an experience I had while working as a volunteer at St George's that I am neither able to explain or forget. It was near Christmas, the Crypt was full. Many of the helpers were young; they seemed to be students and I was new and very nervous. Two of the older visitors, very much under the influence of alcohol, decided to lash into each other with chairs. The Police were called. We carried on handing out sandwiches trying to smile. After a bit the atmosphere eased. A tall elderly man came to me and asked for a pot of tea and 'whatever'.

I could see that he'd been around, but he stood out for different reasons. He had dark eyes and spoke with a soft, quiet voice. He looked to have been a military type and I formed the opinion that he may have been through the war. Although they were well worn, he was dressed in collar and tie. I handed him a pot of tea and turned round to get him a sandwich off a table behind me. When I turned back, he placed his pot of tea on the work surface between us and took hold of my hand. 'Thank you Sir' he said, and he shook my hand long. He looked me straight in the eyes and I knew he meant what he was saying. Then he just walked off towards the wooden benches and sat down. I thought all night about what he'd said. A lot just took without speaking, but he was different. I have thought long and hard over the years about my experiences in the pit, at the morgue during the time of the Yorkshire Ripper and about this man in worn out clothes. It's about brotherhood and faith, is as near as I can get.

☐ There is an old joke, which suggests a volunteer misheard the question! Be that as it may, volunteers do indeed come from all walks of life and for many different reasons, but all share a desire to help people in desperate need, even if we are unsure what this requires and whether we are equal to it.

My own involvement started one Lent. I wanted to do something extra instead of giving something up. That something was spending a couple of evenings alongside the then Crypt Warden, the Rev Don Paterson, and he invited me to become a volunteer one evening a week. So what starts with deciding not to give up chocolate, but doing something useful turns out to be the longest Lent on record. I'm still here twenty-five years on!

☐ One night one of the lads took his shoes off and walked away somewhere. When he came back they had been sold as separate items. One person took the shoes and another the laces.

☐ There was one very well meaning boot company who sent us a packing case full of left shoes. They sent a note saying 'Sorry we haven't sent the right shoes'. But they were quite sure that people coming to the Crypt would be glad of the use of one shoe. Of course we weren't able to do much but there we are. People cared.

☐ I admit it. I had been naughty at school. My Grandfather never believed in smacking. He took me by the hand and said 'I'm going to take you somewhere now, because I want to show you something that will make you realise how lucky you are'. He brought me to see the dark benches at the Crypt. Many years after, when my husband died in my arms, I thought my world had dropped in. Then I thought – I'm no good to anybody sitting in the house crying. I increased a commitment I already had to a charity called SCOPE. Six months ago I heard the Rev Gary Stott give a talk about the Crypt. I remembered my Grandfather. I applied to volunteer on a Wednesday morning. A lot of people sit in their homes. A lot would like to have a comfortable home to sit in. Though I must admit, in cold dark weather I'd like to put my head back under the duvet.

Crypt archive

☐ St George's, of course, has a great tradition to keep up for offering hospitality and helping others. We would often respond to notices put out on the pews. We have been able to offer hospitality to many foreign visitors, archdeacons, people from universities. We had a gentleman called Oswald come to stay from Sri Lanka and Lynette from Sarawak came on and off for three years. We still get letters at Christmas and Easter. We felt it our duty as members of the congregation.

☐ I was delivering some clothes to the Crypt office when I became aware of some activity on the grass. Don Paterson, who was Warden at the time, was being held by several clients. They started to bump him up and down, shaking him like a blanket. It was, apparently, Don's birthday and the men were having fun. Don laughed as though this was normal behaviour. It certainly spoke volumes about the way Don interacted and was able to come alongside the clients, not only that but it spoke about the way the men felt about him.

☐ My Mother set an example. She used to give meals to travelling folk; I was used to people around the house. I became interested in helping the vulnerable. As a teenager I was struck by the love, care and compassion shown at the Crypt, though I was not a committed Christian. When I was married I stopped going to the Crypt. When my husband lost his job and found someone else I started a downhill slide into tranquillisers and alcohol. Through one problem after another I ended up at Regent Terrace, the refuge set up by a wonderful couple Francis and Joe. Ironically I had helped decorate the place as a teenager. The love in that place was tangible. The love there sowed the seeds of my conversion in 1982. The Lord has done many wonderful things in my life. I no longer have a drink and tranquilliser problem. I have a new wonderful husband and two more grown up children.

☐ I used to give bread out; I think we allowed three slices. A lot asked for crusts because there's more bread on a crust. With the tea we filled the beaker right to the brim; that was very important.

☐ During the Headingley Test matches, players often came to the church. David Sheppard, who later became Bishop of Liverpool, came to preach and Gary Sobers attended services. Because of the contact I had with Yorkshire Cricket Club they had a warm spot for the Crypt.

One year the match was called off and they had masses of barm cakes over. 'Could I use them?'. I drove up there and loaded my car with barm cakes filled with ham and tongue. No wrapping, an ordinary saloon car full from floor to ceiling and it was a heck of a job. Marks and Spencer once gave us a whole load of Bakewell tarts; the men ate nothing but Bakewell tarts for three days. I couldn't look at the things for ages after that. At Christmas I begged for turkeys, spuds and sprouts. We served over 100 men with all the trimmings.

☐ The usual ration was three slices of white bread, usually some out-of-date stock from a local supermarket. But one evening there was a problem. The bread was brown. The clients of the Crypt were not renowned for their healthy eating and they liked what they knew. We were able to persuade them that on that particular night it was brown or nothing – but they did persuade us to allow them four slices instead of the usual three.

The rest of the evening I spent chatting to the men. It became clear that many of them were in that situation through some kind of family break up. And very often, behind that there was a mental illness.

The evening ended with a short service. Before long I was helping to lead it. Soon the team leader, Les Dawson, discovered that I had a rudimentary ability to pick out notes on a piano. So I was recruited to accompany the hymn. It was the first and last time I have ever played in public. I was probably responsible for the conversion of many of the men to paganism!

We feel comfortable when homeless people fit into the concept of where we think they ought to be.

☐ Jack and me volunteered for six years. It was at the time of the Yorkshire Ripper and there was a lot of fear about. I had a night school job teaching cake decoration at Joseph Priestley College and I picked up Jack at 1 o'clock at night. I also took nurses and staff up to Faith Lodge. Before Christmas the boys from Monkton Combe School at Bath would come up to help distribute toys. On the Golden anniversary of the Crypt I worked throughout Christmas Day to make table decorations for the Boxing Day meal. About sixty volunteers past and present had been invited. I plated everything up, including cutting four hundred pieces of cake. A box covered in icing had been made in the shape of the Crypt doorway; it had a slot in the top and seventy pounds was collected.

☐ All my friends thought I was crackers when I said I was going to volunteer to work at the Crypt. They'd say things like 'Well, you've got a lovely husband, a nice home and two children, why do you want to be among them horrible men?' I didn't know why myself. I went to Church regularly, I was a Sunday School teacher and one day I thought I might try to do social work. The Vicar said to me that a way of testing my commitment would be to volunteer at the Crypt. He said to me 'Doing that would really clear your head about what you want to do'. I came and from the start it was 'Mrs Peacock this', and 'Mrs Peacock that', very polite. You learn a lot of things about life when you're giving out soup and bread. You learn a lot about yourself from people for whom life has been hard. People whose friends and family have dropped them, who don't fit in here and don't fit there, can tell a lot about you.

☐ I was frightened some nights. One man looked at my ring and said 'If you sold that it would keep me for above a fortnight' – I stopped wearing it after that. But I grew very fond of many of the men. One lad called Andrew jumped off a bridge in Albion Street and hurt his feet. He ended up in LGI and I got a call to visit him. Before I could even say anything he asked me for some change for the payphone. Another time I was waiting for a bus to London at Wellington Street coach station. One of the Crypt lads was causing havoc.

He was shouting that he'd been looking after the bus station all night and they wouldn't even give him a drink. He'd been sleeping rough down there. When he saw me he said 'Thanks for coming Betty, all I want is a cup of tea'. Before I got on my bus he tapped me for a fiver. I used to get a bit upset when the Crypt closed for cleaning in the summer. I said 'What are you all going to do?'

☐ There were five of us, two boys and three girls; we kneeled at our Mother's knee to pray. 'Faith gives you strength' she said. In the early years of Tony Waite there was what they call The Key Campaign. A body of students came from Oak Hill Theology College on a mission campaigning for a practical faith and to interest people in Jesus as a living Saviour. They were billeted in the homes of parishioners. We took two ladies in; terrific staunch Christians they were. They taught me a lot about Jesus Christ, how He lived and what He taught. Volunteering to work at the Crypt, and I started doing it more than fifty years ago, was all part and parcel of my faith. I suppose you might say we counselled the men who came here, except they didn't call it counselling in those days, they called it talking to them. That's what we did; we talked to the men.

☐ I have met a lot of very intelligent people here who have come on hard times; one I knew quite well was a Doctor. Others would do anything for drink, some even melted down boot polish. They weren't really allowed in with drink, so I used to try to smell their breath. I won't say I searched them, that would be a bit severe, but I might gently knock up against somebody to see if they had a bottle in their pocket.

☐ You couldn't pull the wool over their eyes all the time even in Don Robins' days, if he smelled beer on your breath he wouldn't let you in; even if you told him that it wasn't your money and that somebody had treated you. He'd say 'I wish somebody would treat me'. He also said 'I'd rather be fooled nine times out of ten, if the odd one makes doing what I do worth it'.

☐ The Boxing Day dinner was one of my favourite days. We might serve up to a hundred men and about three women. The turkeys and the custard were cooked over at the Infirmary.

☐ There is a saying about being a 'fool for Christ'; it means that sometimes in our efforts to do good works we make mistakes. My brother Ted was a Vicar in Middlesbrough. He wrote to me 'Can you look after a young man who wants to come to Leeds until he finds some digs'. I had regularly taken people home for a meal. I saw this as an extension of that. We gave this John a room. At the time I was saving for my holidays and watching every penny. I was also Treasurer of the Freewill Offering, totalling it, recording it and taking it down to Church. John went to Church with us every Sunday, but on this particular Sunday he said he wasn't well and decided to stop in bed. I had nearly £80 saved up for my holidays the following week and John was supposed to find digs before we went away. When we got home from Church the front door was damaged and ajar and some of the rooms were ransacked. There was no sign of John. The police were not long in finding him and he was convicted and sent to prison. I tracked him down to Thorp Arch and visited him to tell him that I forgave; the strongest Christian principle is forgiveness. He told me that he was very sorry for what he had done.

You learn a lot about life when you're giving out soup and bread.

Top:
'Have a Go' A tramping couple
relating experiences
1948

Above:
Wilfred Pickles wishes
'Bon Voyage'
1948

☐ I worked for Welborn's in the 50s. They were up on Cardigan Road, joiners and funeral directors. They're still going today. Our bricklayer was Jack Welborn, a big rough lad, strong as a bull. I was a joiner and my mate was another great big lad called Ernest Hitchin, six foot two and eighteen stone. He could eat half a loaf and dripping for his snap. Ernest was a great practical joker. One day when the boss came round with our wages in a brown envelope, Ernest took his money out and filled the packet up with bits of folded paper and washers. One bloke came shuffling up to the Crypt and saw the wage packet tossed on the floor and bent to pick it up. When Ernest shouted 'Hey up!' to him, he shot off like Jesse Owens. I don't think we did things like that to be cruel. It's just that we were seeing things that we hadn't seen before and I suppose it was how we reacted. There was a young lad who used to come and have a cig and watch us; he never said anything, he just watched. And there was a lot of men who'd dissolved their teeth to little stumps through drinking methylated spirits. It was a gruesome job too. We were building a stoothing wall inside these archways. The stones were as hard as hell and we'd a heck of a job drilling and fastening them. We used Obo nails which had not been out long. Two Home Office men were watching, and re-burying a lot of the remains of the people who had been buried in the Crypt a hundred years before. I remember one coffin. It contained the remains of an eighteen year old girl. The lid was all rotted away. We could see the girl's hair, all long down either side. It still looked perfect and had two combs in it, big combs like they had in Victorian times.

☐ Don Paterson and Richard Allen had real love for these people. They knew that a request for cough medicine was invariably an excuse for a chat. And the work couldn't stop. Often on my night off Don would ring me to come in. If someone wanted a bath the nurse would be forced to leave her station. I would go down and I knew I would be there until after staff prayers at 9 o'clock. The staff might be having difficulties with a schizophrenic, but Don knew how to 'Jolly Jones' in.

☐ There was a doctor up the road who would see the men, but when he retired it was a case of sending them to Casualty. It was around about that time that Dr Keighley started the Medical Service. He had sterling help from a psychologist called Jill Vogler. I believe this was the first practice for down-and-outs in this country. Because of this, if you said you worked or volunteered at the Crypt, the authorities knew what you were talking about. The Crypt was highly respected and taken very seriously.

☐ I used to look forward to the Doctors and Nurses Services every year. The nurses looked beautiful in their navy blue capes with red linings. They wore kerchiefs with *Fal-de-Rals* down the back. The Sisters at Leeds General Infirmary wore pale blue uniforms with lovely white muslin caps perched right on top of their heads.

☐ Dottie Kaufmann was a German who had settled in Tanzania. I had worked at Great Ormond Street. We met when I came to do my 'General' at Leeds. Dottie helped in the Crypt office and we both stayed in the Nurses' Home. It was Dottie who suggested that I volunteer to do nursing duty here. When the fog eventually lifted I could see St George's from where I was. I came across after work. There was a passageway and a little cupboard that had been donated by the boys of Monkton Combe School. They came here to paint and clean in August when the Crypt closed. Inside that cupboard were gallon jars of cough medicine. All the clients coughed when they washed their feet; they did so in that passage in a bowl which was emptied out in the kitchen sink.

☐ Sometimes their toe nails grew right back underneath their toes. An orthopaedic surgeon who volunteered would sometimes work the same evening as me. I would say 'Come on, you're stronger than me, cut these!' They would come here in their rotten and holey shoes and if they were prepared to wash their feet they would be given a clean pair of socks. In Spring-time when the wives of Leeds cleaned out their drawers we had lots of socks given.

I laid in bed and started thinking
'What am I going to do with my life?'

Crypt archive

☐ If the clients came in with scabies, there was a centre near St James's where you could send them with clean clothes and a note. Poor Don Wright, if we were sorting out flea-ridden clothes he would be covered in them – they didn't like my meat. It wasn't everyone's cup of tea of course. There was a lovely young curate who always got on better when talking to students. He couldn't seem to forge a link with the Crypt men. Then there was Brandon Jackson, who seemed to thrive alongside down-and-outs. He used to say 'The only difference between when I go to see them and when the Police go, is that they don't put their fags out when they speak to me'.

☐ I think it was Sharkey or someone who came to fetch me. He trundled me along to an empty house, across broken floorboards to the chimney breast where a fireplace had been and where a fire was blazing made from chopped up floor. A poor old lad was lying there with a fearsome influenza. Sharkey had gone out of his way to find me. Sleeping rough often inspires great loyalty. A lot of the men got quite severe burns too when they fell on makeshift fires. Mick Carroll once got a terribly burned backside. He said 'You see to it Dot, I don't want the young nurses to see my backside'. The alcoholics were my favourites. You knew where you stood with them. Some had T.B., which was a blessing in disguise in a way, because we managed to dry one or two out while they were in Middleton Sanatorium.

☐ Faith Lodge was originally donated to the Crypt as a house for the Crypt Warden, Richard Allen, to live in. It was a big place, so rather than leave part of it empty he started taking the homeless back to live with him. When the Warden moved on, the project kept going. Where we are now was called Hope House, that was where our ladies had been. When the old fashioned vicarage of All Hallows was donated at Regent Terrace, a system developed. The Crypt was where people were first received. These were moved on to Faith Lodge and then on to Regent Terrace, which was like bed-sits, before moving back to regular housing.

☐ The sad death of Don Paterson triggered a review of the whole structure of the Crypt. Up to that point in 1990, and for the previous sixty years, an Anglican Minister had always been in charge of the project. From then on, more professional people with a social work background were brought in. Today Faith Lodge is a 'dry' house where people who are attempting to dry out can live. Regent Terrace is a 'wet' house; it accommodates people who still drink, but they're not allowed to drink in the house. They drink in the garden. Way back in Mr Robins' day he would say 'If they can afford a drink, they can afford somewhere to stay'. When Margaret and I inherited Faith Lodge we reinforced that policy. Faith Lodge has a tremendous reputation as a 24-hour-a-day dry house. If you really want to get dry, there's no better place. We will chase anybody away from the door who our guests don't want to see.

☐ The first morning of my work here I lay in bed and listened to people going past my partly open bedroom window. I came to the curtain and looked into the street. I saw a young West Indian lad on his way past to school. He spoke in a strong, broad Yorkshire accent. I knew I had arrived. In the next few years Margaret and I lived, slept, ate and dreamed the premises. At times our tempers wore very thin. Imagine working alongside your wife and bringing up two teenage daughters in a house full of recovering alcoholics. I bought a mobile home and put it on a campsite to the north of Leeds. I insisted that we take one full 24 hour period off each week. Nowadays we have our own house off the premises and me and my wife wave to one another as we pass on the motorway, at the start and end of our shifts.

☐ The Crypt always closed for the duration of August and reopened on 1 September. One year for refurbishment they decided to close through to January. This was a great upset for the people who called the Crypt their home. On some sharp frosty nights up to 130 people would sleep in there, some even brought their own cardboards in to sleep on. We had to do something for the real square pegs who wouldn't go into round holes. There was about twelve who were completely out of kilter with society, lacking social skills and respect for rules and regulations. We closed down the bedsit project at Regent Terrace and moved them to there.

☐ I'm old fashioned about Christmas. I like to put the trimmings up on Christmas Eve and take them down on Twelfth Night. I don't like cobwebs hanging from them. Christmas has always been a great tradition for us and our two daughters, so when we came here we brought that continuity. We said 'This is our family and we want our guests to be part of it'. We bought Christmas presents for all the guys at Faith Lodge; soap, flannels, toothpaste, underwear, things like that – stuff you might buy for your uncle. Now, one of the guys at Faith Lodge, Lenny, had slept rough for over 40 years at the brickworks on Gelderd Road. Sleeping near kilns was a favourite amongst tramps because they remained warm throughout the night. When the brickworks closed down in the 1980s Lenny found his way to the Crypt and then to here. On this particular Christmas Eve Don Paterson bedded everybody down at the Crypt and then came up here to say good night. 'Where's Lenny?' he asked. We found Lenny up in his room crying. He wouldn't tell us why. This is where the woman's sensitive touch comes in. My wife and daughters talked gently to him. On Boxing Day Lenny told his story. He had once been dapper and handsome and he sang in Upper Armley Church Choir. One Christmas Eve his mother died. He couldn't cope and walked out of the house leaving everything to his sister. This was the first Christmas he'd had a present and a roof over his head since then. These days Lenny is a pain in the butt at Christmas time; as the day approaches he's always asking 'When are the decorations going up?'

☐ Don Paterson phoned me and said 'We've got a guy down here, can you take him for Christmas?' I knew a bit about Dickson Little: ex Army Sergeant Major, came out and couldn't adjust to civvy life, heavy drinker, hard fighter. 'OK Don, we'll give him a try'. We'd already bought everybody presents, and budgets being budgets there wasn't much left, but I found a brand new Aran jumper at the Crypt, so I wrapped that up for him. He lasted two months without a drink after that before he went off. He made a second appearance and lasted a month. After that I didn't hear about him for ages. Years later I get a phone call from a lovely guy called Charlie down at the Whitehall Road resettlement unit. 'I've got Dick Little here – he wants to come home to die'. I was stunned and said 'Back up a bit, what's the story'. It turns out that he's had major lung surgery and he's not getting any better. What can I do, we're not medical people and we have no medical facilities? I took him in and agreed with the Macmillan nurses that they would make regular visits and the Wheatfields Hospice would take him during the last days. A local G.P. was very supportive. Dickson had hallucinations. He ran away from people who weren't chasing him. The police found him in Chapeltown and brought him home. Wheatfields took him and he went missing again. We found him delirious in the Arndale Shopping Centre. He wasn't going to take death lying down. I found he had a sister on the outskirts of Newcastle. I explained the situation and she came down here to stay for the weekend. On the Sunday, out of the blue, his sister said 'I'm taking him back with me'. A doctor said 'The state he's in, it won't make a difference'. On the Tuesday the sister rang to say he had passed on. All that time he had clung on to his Aran sweater. All that time of needing money to buy a drink he had refused to sell it; he wouldn't part.

☐ What you've got to realise with alcoholics is that these guys don't drink for enjoyment like you or I might do. There is a bottom line somewhere, a foundation. You have to knock all the bricks down that they have built around themselves to get down to this foundation. I have helped RAF Squadron Leaders, top scientists; alcoholism is in all walks of life. Nobody knows for sure what causes it. Some say alcoholism is in genetic make up, others say it is triggered by something. I knew a man called Snowy – he was called that because of his hair – even the police knew him as Snowy. He saw the horrors in a concentration camp. I know that is what triggered him. If I was told that they had discovered a cure for alcoholism in Harrogate, I would have my guests on their hands and knees queuing to get there.

☐ There was an advert in *The Buzz*, a Christian magazine. That's what brought me here to Faith Lodge. Previous to that I had visited the Crypt because of its famous reputation. We were ferried to and from St George's from our digs at Regent Terrace in a yellow van. The van had no windows, and I had no idea where I was going, no picture of Leeds. The real reason I ended up here was the closure of a rehab unit for alcoholics I ran in Plymouth. At the monthly Trustees' meeting I was told I was on a month's notice. It was a traumatic time. I was dealing with guys with severe problems. I had just four weeks to find places for 15 men in other hostels. One of the guys had a 'wet' brain. He had been a pub landlord and one day he walked in to a pub and began serving drinks. He ended up in a psychiatric hospital.

☐ The social workers wanted me to go and live with an old lady as a companion. When you're just 16 you don't want it. So I said 'No'. They took me to St George's Crypt House at Wellclose Place. I paid two quid a week board from my wage as a winder at Johnsons Mill on Kirkstall Road. One day Mrs Dean, the plump woman who looked after the place, knocked on my door and stood with a plateful of tab ends. We weren't allowed to smoke, but I'd been smoking out the window and all the tabs and other stuff had landed on top of her bay window.

☐ People don't realise how poor you can get. When you're desperate and you've got kids you forget pride. It's not easy going begging for a Christmas tree lit up with lights, but I've been pleased to do it, just to see the kiddies' faces.

☐ He was a good husband at first, but when he had the drink in him he lashed out. Then he'd want to make babies. He got to the stage where he slept all day and went wandering about at night. One morning he screamed at me and told me that if I was in the house when he came back in he'd kill me and the children. I was at the end of my wits. I took all my five children to the police station. The policeman said 'You should be back at home with your husband'. I had read about the Crypt so I went there. It was the middle of the morning. All we had was the clothes we stood up in and I hadn't packed the kids' pyjamas; I even told them to leave their toys. They took me to a safe house which was looked after by two lovely ladies. I loved cleaning up and doing, so I helped them to strip beds and wash clothes. It's all such a long time ago now, my lad is in his forties and he'd only be about ten at the time. Some days though, when I have to go for an appointment at the Infirmary, I look over at the Crypt and think of all the kindness.

☐ We could only sleep 27 and we often had to turn over 100 away. They would go off to the old houses that hadn't been pulled down yet. The men called them 'skips' as in a place to kip in and the lads who slept there were 'skippers'. It was heartbreaking sometimes to have to turn them away. In the main they were very interesting people. For six or nine months we housed a famous clown. He gave a performance for the men at the Boxing Day meal. When people ask 'Why do you keep going back to the Crypt?', I tell them I'm hooked. Why do people keep taking heroin?

Certainly, I know fewer answers now than when I started to volunteer.

One of the criticisms people used against the night shelter was that it encouraged people to stay homeless. In my opinion you don't cure homelessness by putting a roof over somebody's head. You have to deal with the deep-rooted problem that caused the homelessness in the first place. Don Paterson knew that too. In the old days anyone who slept at the Crypt for more than three consecutive nights had to have a chat with Don. Slowly, slowly over a period of time the real problem would come out. It's about trust. People don't trust you because you feed them. They don't trust you because you know their name. They come to trust you when they get to know you. In these days of referrals, when people are placed in a hostel or B&B and then moved on to another place the trust isn't there. It's one thing to identify a person, it's another to identify the problem.

In 1982 I worked as a doctor's receptionist in Pudsey. Dr Dorothy Darnborough was there; she worked as a Medical Officer at the Crypt. The cream of the Leeds medical profession came to the Crypt. I was talking to her one day and she said 'Why don't you volunteer?' My good friend Molly Hillam, who was a Moravian like me, came here too; we were a team. We arrived as near to 7 o'clock as we could and we'd socialise for an hour before serving soup. Because of my background I volunteered to work on the medical records. Friday night was like party night when Marks & Spencers fetched sandwiches that would be stale if left unsold.

I had to stop coming when Molly died. It wasn't the same; she was killed one Sunday lunch-time by a car coming down from Pudsey. She was a very talented potter, and just getting well known. Don Paterson came to her funeral, and then a few weeks after, he died. It was such a sad time.

One Monday we were standing in the kitchen up at Faith Lodge and Don Paterson asked me 'What part of Liverpool are you from?' I told him that it was Speke. He said that he had been a Curate there and went on to ask me where I lived. I told him Harland Green. He told me that he and some others held prayer meetings in a house in Harland Green and that they often prayed for some local kids who kicked a ball against the wall. We put two and two together and worked out that one of those kids was me. In the years between I had been homeless, a drunk, a Crypt client, and now I was working alongside a man who all those years before had said prayers for me. You could call it coincidence, but I don't like that. I know that Don took great encouragement from the knowledge that his prayers were answered.

Some people have the mistaken idea that if someone is homeless or in bed and breakfast accommodation, they'll be grateful for anything.

Reportage Photography
John Angerson

Poetry workshop

Sleep

I've slept on building sites and
in hayfields
I've slept under curtains
and cardboards
I've slept in the rain
and out of the rain
I've slept behind a bush one day
and in a park
I've slept in bus stations
and heard commotions
I've dreamed of dogs and seen
packs of men
I've seen the eighteenth century
And now I can take sleeping tablets
'cos I don't sleep so well.

Untitled

Every day somebody is pulling
dirty strokes
It starts the minute you walk
Out of the door.
In this world certain people try
To humiliate you.
They want to be superior
They live on superiority
I live on the street
They thrive on it
Sooner or later it will happen to you.

Joblessness and alcoholism were once the main causes of poverty which the Crypt was set up to alleviate. The issues now are wider; drug taking, childhood abuse, damaged personalities, psychiatric disorders deemed treatable outside of institutions, stress with an increasingly bureaucratic world, loss of domestic stability, oppressive estates of poor housing and refugees from war-torn states worldwide. The Crypt, now spacious, bright and professionally run as a Charity, remains determined to uphold its tradition of helping the vulnerable.

Voices in this final part talk about the Crypt today. Here are some stories by poets, teachers, reformed alcoholics, a man who sells the *Big Issue*, a retired magistrate, an architect, a builder and the current Rector. There are heart warming tales from a young single mother returning to education and a student who has found a vocation here.

'... Thou perhaps under the whelming tide
Visit'st the bottom of the monstrous world;
Look homeward angel now...'
John Milton

Part Three

... And poor is still here today

1990 – Now

This is a very special place. My own memories of it begin in 1959 when I came to live in Little Woodhouse. St George's then still had its spire and Clarendon Road ran right up to its gates. Some of my neighbours were parishioners and others were volunteers. Other neighbours included users of the Crypt, accepted as part of the neighbourhood mostly without question. I can only recall one instance of intolerance when an ill-advised local politician whipped up a summer storm of indignation when campaigning for the Crypt's closure.

Since as long ago as the 17th Century the people of this area have striven to help others less fortunate than themselves. Leighton Street, across the road from the Crypt, commemorates Isabel Leighton, who left a charity to help educate poor children. A scholarship in her name still helps less well-off students at Leeds University. Dr Heaton, whose grave is the last one in the Churchyard, promoted education for women as well as men in the 19th Century and his sister Ellen, who lived in Woodhouse Square, showed the spirit of practical kindness, later echoed by Don Robins, when she paid for working men to have a good tea before they went on to night school.

The Little Woodhouse people who built St George's in 1838 had in mind not only the spiritual welfare of middle class people in pleasant villas, but the needs of poor workers in the crowded streets along Park Lane. In the 1960s and 70s along with the demolition of the slums we saw the relentless spread of University and Hospital departments. The ancient hamlet of Little Woodhouse disappeared under the Dental School. Our neighbourhood has become a very different place. The pleasant villas have become University and Hospital departments, bail hostels, as well as addiction and psychiatric units, dealing with the many problems of modern life. Students have replaced permanent residents in the smaller Victorian terraces now owned by absentee landlords. The old streets off Park Lane and the back-to-backs have been replaced by Council estates and some new private housing. The construction of the Inner Ring Road divorced us from the City and almost made us a secret suburb. The footbridge over the motorway maintains our only link with St George's.

In the early 90s when politicians were denying the existence of society, we formed the Little Woodhouse Community Association. We seek to continue the local spirit of care and helping others by improving our neighbourhood for those who live and work here. With help from St George's Community Development Officer, Peter Green and willing church volunteers, we have run events such as the Hanover Square Festival and the Claremont Streets Centenary when many older residents were reunited. Today, in the area around St George's, further changes have come. 'City living' is now in the lofts of Centaur House and Denison Hall. Schools and offices are fast being converted in this new trend to house the wealthy. Alongside, and mixed in with this, are student block money spinners, the bail hostels and the psychiatric units. We, the residents, are still here too. This heady mix of rich and poor, educational privilege and disadvantage, high flyers and unemployed in Little Woodhouse is perhaps a snapshot of modern-day society. A constant part of this for over 70 years through all the changes is St George's Crypt. Going forward bravely in an attempt to help those in most need, it is an example to us all. It's not perfect, but I would like anyone who can do better to step forward.

☐ I try to invest time and energy when I can have impact, and although I would have loved to spend more time on the Crypt's Business Committee, after a time I felt that I was most use as someone who could network and bring a range of outside resources to the organisation. I work in this way because I am committed to a better, more inclusive Leeds. I don't agree that this is a two-speed city. We are all bound together in a complex way. We have a common history, economy, environment, social structure and a future which I believe can be nurtured to produce a more just and reasonable community.

It is easy to be negative about the people who spend some of their time at the Crypt.I think that I am a realist and this makes me see that we have to recognise that in the modern city, where the pace of life can be hectic and erratic, at one point you can be riding high and another sunk low; the Crypt and similar organisations have a necessary function. At best they give people whose lives might have drifted towards chaos for a number of reasons, a chance to adjust and find a way through.

My particular interest is in housing and the environment but that can never stand alone. Recently I became interested in the development of the Supertram because I see it as a development which will draw people back into the city centre. Isolation in vast estates which offer very little beyond basic housing, where there are no shops or natural places to come together for recreation, where crime and unemployment have fed off each other, has been a disaster. The city centre is beginning to breathe again.

I cite that transport example because it affects how we will live in a decade's time, but I could focus elsewhere. My working life for the last ten years has been concerned with regeneration and I can tell you that the problems seen in the urban core which includes the Crypt must be visible and are part of the fabric of our life. Local action zones have been identified on the outskirts, so must not sweep perceived problems into the suburbs but recognise them as a part of the way city life evolves. If we are to retain our position as one of the fastest moving cities in the country then we have to take a wide view and see to it that everyone gets something out of the development process and no one is left to rot.

☐ People will tell you that the Crypt is and was for down-and-outs and folk with alcohol and drug problems. It's for the poor. I suffered the indignity of going to school in women's ATS shoes and old army battle dress. I rubbed my fingers raw pulling coal off the stacks at the University. Pinching but necessary. I got chits from Boots for the bairns; that's poor and poor is still here today.

☐ There is a time when you need to shout from the rooftops and another time to go and see people through connections. When I was Bishop of London I went with Basil Hume to see John Gummer. We wanted to discuss the Conservative Party's policy on homeless people. I believe we had an effect. At the time we had a Diocesan officer for the homeless. I said to him one day that I would like to go on his rounds with him. He said 'Meet me at the Tottenham Court Road Tube station'. We went to the Lincoln's Inn Field squat and had a humorous encounter with a glue-sniffing chap who had a pet rat called Adolf. It ran up and down his arm and he was kissing it. We were offered a cup of tea; I'm fairly sure I didn't drink it. Between two and three o'clock in the morning we found ourselves on Charing Cross Road. I had a conversation with an intelligent young man in a shop doorway. He kept himself clean and by day was a regular library user. At about 11.30 that morning I attended a Lord Mayor's luncheon at The Guildhall. I looked around the hall thinking 'Am I in the same world?'.

A pat on the hand here and a hand on the shoulder there is just as important as showing somebody how to spell a difficult word.

☐ I slept rough from a very early age after my parents threw me out; they were real bastards to me. I never went to school, and then one day I became curious. I had gone to see *Snow White and the Seven Dwarfs* in a local cinema in Edinburgh. It cost one shilling in the cheap seats from what I remember. I watched the film over and over again, through all performances, and when the lights went out for the last time I didn't go out of the cinema but settled down for the night. I was awoken by a cleaner who crept up and frightened me to death. 'Why didn't you leave last night?' she said. 'I didn't know how to; I couldn't see which door I was to go out of'. 'Well, it's quite clear, it says Exit'. 'I don't know what exit means and I can't read' I said.

She pointed to the door and I took out a pencil which I kept with me and some old pieces of paper. I wrote the shapes of the letters down as she watched. Then she said something which changed my life. 'If you can learn that word by next Friday, I'll pay for you to go into the cinema myself'. It was Tuesday then. By the Friday I had written the word down 100 times and in the months that followed I took to writing down any words that I could see in the street: *Dangerous; level crossing; gentlemen; trains; railway station*. Every time I saw a new word I would go up to a person, tell them that I could not read and get them to say the word to me, then watch me as I wrote it down. In the end my parka, that was an old sort of coat, had its pockets filled with lists and lists of words.

As time passed I began to be more confident. That lasted until one morning when I saw a man sitting reading the *Daily Mirror*. I went up to him and said 'Would you listen to me read the front page?' He said he would and I struggled through it. When I couldn't say a word he told me what I had missed out and I was surprised by just how much I could read. It was then that I saw words-within-words. Gentle-men had two parts. Later somebody said 'Why don't you go to the library?' I said 'What's a library?' But eventually I got there for I love books, though I have never owned one in my life.

Brahm Design

Above:
St George's Crypt
2002

Now I write poetry. I think I have written 17,000 poems but a lot of them got burnt when I was sleeping rough in Cardiff and someone set fire to my sleeping bag. In those days I had a lot of them in loose-leaf files but I now carry them with me. One of my recent ones is called *Bob from Bolton*. It goes on for thirteen pages and tells the story of a politician who got votes by giving people black pudding. He also sets up a zoo before he is poisoned.

I am always on the move, although I do have a flat in Leeds. I scoff a lot of fish and chips in my time and go all over. I regularly pass over the Pennines to Preston, but I've been as far as the Shetlands, Swansea and beyond, and to the bottom of Cornwall via Plymouth.

The word I will never forget is *Exit*, because it started me off. Nor will I forget the cleaning lady at the cinema and the Joe Normal man who helped me to read the front page of his newspaper.

☐　I have got my own place; I live up by an Off Licence in Chapeltown. Each morning I walk up to St Aidan's where I have a talk with the Vicar – I don't know his name – and then have a loaf of bread, some beans and some tea. That done I go down to the Job Centre looking for work. Five years ago I was working regularly at a garden centre but when that ended I was prepared to take anything that was on offer, tidying up, doing gardens, that sort of thing but couldn't get much. Now I am not in permanent work.

I always come to the Crypt in the evenings, get some food and then wander back after I have had a chat and probably played a game of dominoes with Phil and some of the others. I like being by myself, I like being quiet, so when the Crypt closes I walk back home, have a small lager and then go to bed.

☐　We have a transient lifestyle here. There's not much structure to our lives but many of us see things in a different way and get on with that, which is different from most people's. Personally I don't bother with beer, though a lot do. My enthusiasms are music and motor bikes.

Poetry means a lot to me because it allows me to express my inner self. As I see it, I am a very different type of poet to those who have gone before. When Byron, Mary Shelley and the others sat around discussing horror stories and putting together the story which later developed into *Frankenstein* they were up in the mountains away from the world. I am not, but very much in the thick of things. Poetry is always a solitary occupation, but unlike them I come from a different class so cannot afford to be over-indulgent. They were the children of aristocrats and philosophers. I am Glaswegian working class, though I tell people I only put the accent on for a bit of a laugh, and I'm proud to be of that culture.

Quite naturally, my poetry is different from theirs. My inspiration comes less from the poets of the past; WB Yeats, Keats and people like that, and more from the songwriters of today and of my youth. *Lucy In The Sky With Diamonds*, part drugs, part nonsense, was one of the first songs/poems to get to me. What I like about it is that it is taking the piss out of the English language and, as someone who is dyslexic, that appeals.

Most of my verse gets written down, but some I can recite:

> *I got up on half past Thursday*
> *And went downstairs to get a bite*
> *I opened the fridge door*
> *And the fridge said to me.*

I have another one called Ode to a *Small Green Blob of Putty found under my Armpit one Summers Night*. Are you getting the idea?

☐ I see Llewellyn tramping up and down the lane now with a bottle of cheap vodka hanging out of his sports jacket pocket. He's been wearing the same shirt for at least six months; it's one of those striped ones with a plain white collar, the sort business men wore in the 1970s. At the time when he was still allowed in pubs we spent happy hours listening to his dry banter and outrageous ditties. For a long time the most surrealistic afternoon I ever spent was in Llewellyn's company. It started when Lew announced 'Arnold, when I look at you I often think about euthanasia being a good option'. Arnold, who had returned from a boozy trip to Snaith and misheard him replied 'Well, tha could have come with us, there was room on the bus'. Lew looked around, made eye contact with four or five others round the bar and said 'See what I mean. Simple!' 'Nay, I'm not simple! Joe's simple. You ask him'. Joe was the man who once wrote to Guinness demanding royalties after being led to believe they were using his image on advertising. What was never explained to him was that the darts and dominoes team carried a poster they had made, from one pub to another, putting it on the wall just before Joe arrived. Lew's conversation with Arnold spun off in opposite directions of the compass, until by 3 o'clock Lew was on to how many ready meals he had in his freezer and Arnold was reminiscing about his days as Loft Manager for the Perry Brothers' pigeon racing team. It was shortly after this that some of us who were witness to the conversation formed the Salvador Dali Club 'for rogues, fakirs, braggarts, liars and those who believed their giraffe was on fire'. We met the second Sunday of every month to drink Campari and soda and organise trips to unsuspecting country pubs.

I said that for a long time this was the most surreal conversation I had ever listened to. Now I have one to top it. It happened on a Friday afternoon at the Crypt as people were coming to try on new clothes. Around the table were Peter, Arthur, Harry, Jimmy and Billy, and the conversation went something like this: 'When Jersey Joe Walcott fought Rocky Marciano they begged the referee to let it go one more round'. 'Was that when Jerry Lee Lewis was fighting?'
'No, he played piano'.
'There was a man called Chick Fowler. He was a fighter. He sold Old Moores Almanac outside Lewis's. There was always a page or two missing. He sold Old Moore by instalments'.
'Archie Moore'
'Who?'
'Archie Moore. He was another good 'un!'
'There were these three Italian prisoners of war. One of them, I think they called him Francisco, let me watch that Marciano fight on his little telly'. 'I saw it at Bondi Beach Bar – that's what they call it now. It wasn't that then'.
'Beware of men telling you a soft story young man'. Soft story it wasn't. Entertaining, funny, downright dippy, but not soft. I don't really know what to make of it. And it doesn't have the same impact on the page as when I first heard it. Perhaps instead of creative writing we should instigate classes in creative talking.

When you first stop drinking you count. You count the hours, then you count the days, the weeks, the months and eventually the years.

☐ I didn't start drinking till I was 29. When I went to the NAAFI I'd ask for a glass of milk. The lads would laugh at me and shout 'Cissy'. I just laughed it off and said 'We'll see in the morning when the man blows his bugle'. The next day they'd be trying to get their straps and buckles together asking me to help them. 'Who's the frigging Cissy now then eh?'

My brother bought me a pint of Olde English Cider. I thought it was a baby drink, but sure, that was a lovely drink. After half an hour I needed another and so it goes. In the morning instead of coffee I took a glass of cider. I don't know when I started boxing surgical spirit into the cider. The skippers call it White Lady, the only time you smell it is when you piss or sweat. If you box it in to beer, the beer goes white; if you box it to coca-cola that goes white; only the orange juice stays the same colour. Many times I have had four orange juices in a bar and the landlord has wondered why I've staggered out. I'll tell you, I never got a cough or cold when I drank the Lady. I've slept in the roughest places and the lice won't come near, neither will the long tails (that's rats). Open a bottle of wine on a wall and you might have every bee in the world round you. Now 'the Blue', that's meths, is a great livener. You might take Tyson on or climb Mount Everest in your swimming trunks when you've had three shots of that. The drinking school I was in didn't like the meths. If they knew you'd been drinking it they'd say 'Don't pass the wine to him!'. Bel-Air women's hairspray was the other – you could squeeze a sachet of that into cider. I didn't care, but it became a routine. A few mates, cider and White Lady, a derelict house and lay down after a few bottles. Then it was like the Waltons.
'If I see you in the morning I'll see you.'
'Don't shed a tear for me if I'm dead.'
'No, and don't cry for me.'
'You'll let my family know.'
'Goodnight.'

One day in Manchester I was sick. I thought it was red wine but it was blood. A traveller girl called Winnie who looked after me got me to hospital. They had to give me a transfusion. I remembered all the little nips I took when I worked as a kitchen porter, the skippering and the White Lady. There's no magical cure. You can have the implants like George Best, but you can take them out. *Emeneferen*, they don't give them out now. Only does the job of a livener. *Librium* is alright, it helps you with the shakes and then there's *Antibuse*, but I don't believe in tablets. It's in the mind. You will cure yourself if you can get right in your mind. I achieved what I wanted to achieve with drinking. Some enjoyment as well. Now I can enjoy myself without it. I can buy my daughter a £30 pair of trainers; it's what I would have spent on nine bottles, and I can still have the *craic*.

OK, you've got two days
to find £600 back rent or
you are out on the street ...
and you're skint.

Brahm Design

Above:
K2 Building Development
2002

☐ OK. You've got two days to find £600 back rent or you are out on the street. You're skint. You've got some possessions; lap-top, art materials, a bass guitar, a midi-hifi, perhaps you could sell them; but most of them are precious things that you want to hold on to. If you can find perhaps £200, you might have the deposit on a new flat. The DSS tells you that a hostel is an option. I'll tell you the truth. I managed to stash most of my things with friends and with a 60 quid sleeping bag I went onto the street. The great irony was I'd survived heroin addiction while maintaining a home, and now I was clean I was out on my arse. It's the big trap. I was penalised for honesty basically. I was working part-time and claiming housing benefit. They cut off my money and I didn't appeal within the 28-day rule. Three months down the line I owe my landlady 600 quid and she wants me out. I appealed to logic. Logic can sometimes be too simple for the machinery of Government bureaucracy. It would have cost them less to help me pay my back rent than to put me in a hostel – too simple that, too elegant a solution. I approached my homelessness in a practical way. I'm an organised person. I learned to support myself while at public school. I'd arrived there as a South London scholarship boy with an accent like something out of *Lock, Stock and Two Smoking Barrels.* I was alienated by the posh boys. You quickly learn to support yourself when you're alienated.

You learn to be polite on the streets, it's less hassle. If a private security guard or a policeman moves you on from the Town Hall steps or a doorway near Lillywhites Sports, it's no good being rude. Be polite and just one time, they might leave you to get some sleep. I know very few people on the streets for whom 'it's all their own fault', but you are made to feel it is by many people; especially drunken people. For some reason the sight of a homeless person annoys and offends a lot of people who are rolling to their homes drunk.

I manage most days to get a shower and dry clothes down at St Anne's Day Centre, and human contact and food at St George's Crypt. St George's is a place where you can spend three hours in the evening, getting warm, engaging in conversation, smoking and drinking tea; simple pleasures. I can't underestimate the importance of proper budgeting when you're on the street, because effectively you're eating out every day.

☐ When you stay for the night with a lot of different friends, you soon run out of friends. Then there are some who'll say 'Come on friend, you can come back to my house and sleep on the sofa'. You can't sleep for fear that they will do something to you. And even if they did you can't report them, because when they know you are nobody, they know you can't go to the police.

☐ I pinched stuff, like a lot of teenage girls would, who had nowhere to live and no money. And eventually I ended up at Ripon House Probation Hostel. We were sent out from nine in the morning until half past five to look for work. It was that right hot summer in 1976 so we spent more time larking about than knocking on factory doors. When the colder days came we used to go to the library and tell people we were students studying philosophy at Leeds University and they'd go 'Oh! Yes, course you are!'. We had mates who went to the Crypt for cups of tea and cigs; nobody asked what you did there. In the end I got a job washing up upstairs at Wimpy... some bloody philosophy student!

☐   I went from a children's home to that hostel up Beeston and then to free cups of coffee from some people who dished it out near the Merrion Centre. Then I ended up going to the Crypt. At least people listened to you there. I was nearly 20 before anybody listened to me.

☐   You've got to be homeless, transient or in a hostel to get badged up. I buy my *Big Issue* for 40 pence at the office near the Palace Pub and sell it for a quid. It's like running a small business. I try to target people who are working in town, the shoppers are usually fed up of being asked six or seven times already if they'd like to buy one. *Waterstones* has been a good pitch for me, because you know people who go there already like to read. Some of the sellers do get up to tricks to try to sell the paper. We had one who we nicknamed 'Last Issue Lee'; he always claimed that he was trying to sell his last paper, and then he'd pull another out. The *Big Issue* is one of the best things that could have happened. It really pisses me off when I see negative publicity, it does nobody any favours when I hear that 'All *Big Issue* sellers are smack-heads and scum'.

☐   This is how easy it is to end up sleeping out. I went to a Wishbone Ash concert at Leeds Uni. I was told that if I wasn't in by 11 p.m. I would be locked out. At midnight I was still in Leeds city centre eating a kebab. I ended up back at the house of some mates drinking wine and smoking dope until 4 o'clock in the morning. I kipped on their floor. The following morning I got talking to a bloke who'd just got the keys for a Council house and wanted a lodger. I went home, had a row with my family for stopping out all night and told them I was moving out. For a while things went well at the Council house. We had two chairs, a table, a settee where the springs stuck in your arse and a mattress each to sleep on. The back bedroom window iced up when the winter came and I traced the pattern of ferns on the inside of the pane. I never missed a week's rent money. What I didn't know was that my 'landlord' was putting my rent money with his half of it and spending it in *The Ship Inn*. After a while the Council were on our backs for hundreds of quid. It caused a right old row between us.

The rift widened even more, when he came home early one Saturday and caught me in the bath with a woman he had brought home a couple of times. We ended up having a bit of a punch up and I was told to get out. I couldn't face going back home with a rucksack full of unwashed clothes and an armful of LPs, so I crashed with three different mates in three nights. Come the weekend I found myself outside of a nightclub, drunk, skint and on my own. I started walking out into the countryside and as the sun was just coming up I fell asleep under a big old conker tree. The rain woke me. I was hung over and shivering, and for the first time since I'd been a kid I wanted my Mam and somewhere to clean my teeth. I brushed my hair with my fingers in a pub lavatory. When I looked in the mirror my face was filthy and my eyes were red and bleary. I was just 19 years old and I started to cry. The next night I slept in a barn full of old straw and had nightmares about rats and dirty clothes.

On the Monday I went to work as normal and avoided questions about what I'd done at the weekend. I took to going back to work late at night and sleeping on some sacks in the storeroom. I was due in court the following week charged with possession of cannabis. There's nothing worse than telling a magistrate 'I have no fixed abode' – anybody will tell you that. After asking for social reports, the magistrates sentenced me to three months in a Young Offenders prison. On your first day in those places you are given a small Bible with tissue-thin pages. A lot of the lads use the pages to roll cigarettes with. I tried it three or four times, but I couldn't bring myself to do it after that. There's something very seedy about crushing old tab ends up in a page from the Gospel of St Luke. When I came out of nick an angel took me in. She was an elderly lady who the Social Services relied on to take waifs and strays. She didn't ask for anything apart from rent money on time, that I made the bed and kept the room tidy and that I didn't lose my house key. I kept it on a leather string round my neck. Phoebe was a shining angel. Places like St George's Crypt provide soup and bread and somebody to talk to. But it's the angels who volunteer to take on the bad lads, the misunderstood and the down who bring you back up again.

☐ I sometimes think that the people I meet in the Crypt are the priests and prophets of our age, the flies in the ointment. Anyone who lives in a modern city knows that things are not quite right and their very existence is a call for us to open our ears, hearts and minds. In the Old Testament the prophets Isaiah, Amos and Ezekiel spoke of God's nature but also railed on about the decadence of the community. These women and men who come to us bring with them not only a hint of God himself, but show that society is not working as it should.

When I was younger I had to reconcile my interest in Theology with Faith and the practice of the Christian life. I could not quite get the three-fold balance right. The history of the Church sometimes helped me for I quickly realised that God had called me, as he had called St Francis, to be a new fool. Thinking about it the emphasis was on new, for like Francis I found myself seeking God and yet standing in new environments where the needs of the poor and dispirited were not being met. The Bible told me that 'the Word could become flesh and pitch its tents among us'. I still like that translation. 'Pitch its tents' is a resounding phrase for it emphasises place and the place to which I have been drawn is St George's Crypt, Leeds.

I know that we do not have the answers to deal with problems we meet here. We are striving. The paternalism of the Victorians is not right for this age – nor are the business skills which have developed to satisfy the needs of people who wish to express Christian charity in gifts and service – but I do know that there must be a solution. It possibly lies somewhere in the co-dependency of all of us who come to the Crypt. We must learn to listen to each other's voices and if in the first instance this means that we have to break the bonds that are at the moment binding us together then that must happen. New growth can then take place. At the beginning when I was a student things seemed clearer than they do now, for today I know I am not the solution to homelessness in Leeds. No one personality can tackle a problem of that magnitude, but neither can any sort of institution. Like others here I am still searching.

One thing, however, is certain. I will find the solution in listening, for I truly believe that the Word was made flesh. I just have to listen carefully and watch so that I can understand the meaning of that verse in John's Gospel. I must also look carefully. When I first came to the Crypt I found a painted fresco and on it phrases from the Psalms. A bird was shown flying over the centre of Leeds above the Town Hall, the University, the gas works and prison at Armley, and beneath the image of flight and locality *We have escaped like a bird from the snare of the fowler, the snare has been broken and we are set free*.

One night I was working on the files in the office when one of the men came in and stopped me, needing to talk. I am trying to be truthful, so I will admit that that night I was relishing the kudos of being shattered doing God's work. I broke off from what I was doing, I talked a little, I made him a drink and then I said 'Finish your coffee and go to bed, I have work to do'. He went immediately without a fuss but as I worked on still very, very tired I was aware of music being played in another part of the building. I got up and eventually located him sitting in the chapel. The tune he was playing was one we often sing with the older men and women. 'Amazing Grace, how sweet the sound, that saved a wretch like me'. That experience retold me of the Grace of God.

Sometimes we sing a hymn, which goes to the tune *Danny Boy*. I always enjoy it when the men drop the words of the hymn and sing the lines of the old song which they learned in school; *Oh Danny boy, the pipes the pipes are calling, from glen to glen and down the mountain side*. It reminds me that we are all journeying home together.

☐ The first time I met Alexis she staggered into the Family Centre, pushing a brand new pushchair and offering it for sale. She had returned from Worcester and wanted to find a flat in Leeds. She was certain that a hostel would not do, even though she needed to be cared for even then. No, she was not an alcoholic but suffered from Huntington's chorea, a genetic illness from which she had seen members of her family die. This disease affects a sufferer's reasoning powers as well as causing physical problems. Alexis was determined she would not end up in a wheelchair and decided moving from place to place would keep her mobile. She escaped (her words) from accommodation during the night, even when staying with her sister.

Family Centre staff cared for her for 18 months. We helped her furnish a flat; combed the tangles out of her beautiful long auburn hair; showered her; collected her from police stations when she got lost; took abuse from her when she wanted her own way and we wouldn't co-operate; bought her cigarettes; liaised with the Benefits Agency so that she could immediately reclaim her money when she came back from Worcester, which she visited regularly. Penny spent most of her time on a placement with us cleaning her neglected flat. It was becoming evident that Alexis needed more care and a Nursing Home was found for her that specialised in her condition. She regularly left the Home during the night and walked several miles into Leeds to be at the Family Centre for 10 a.m.

She also realised a lifetime ambition to learn to ride. This was arranged by the owner of the Nursing Home and Sally, Family Centre Manager, was invited along to take photos. She loved to attend the Fellowship Group on a Thursday and when asked to choose a favourite hymn she would say she liked them all.

She carried the Crypt's address and phone number in her haversack and we looked after her Will – she had been a competent business-woman before she became ill and still tried to keep her affairs in order. In the end, her mind became more clouded and reports of her lying down on the Headrow for a 'rest' became more frequent. She asked me to buy her a map of England, because she couldn't remember the way to Worcester any more. The last time we saw her, she was staggering away from the Crypt with her haversack and the map.

A few days later, a phone call came telling us of her death. She was just 39. She had been hit by several lorries on the A1 in the south of England. She was identified by the card with her name and the Crypt address that was in her haversack. She had spoken of suicide if her condition worsened, and we will never know if she deliberately walked across the A1, but I think she was just disorientated and didn't realise where she was.

Her mother and one of her sisters attended the funeral in St George's and were overwhelmed by the number of people present – almost a hundred past and present Crypt staff; staff from the Nursing Home; friends amongst the Crypt clients; a worker from the local sandwich shop and others whose lives had been touched by her unique personality. I shall always be grateful to have known her. She enriched our lives and the life of the Family Centre and the Night Centre, even though she was frustrating; sometimes loving; sometimes aggressive. If I see someone with long auburn hair hanging loose, I remember Alexis and say 'Thank you for her, Lord'.

☐ There are happy endings. Geoff was brought into the Crypt one night by some other clients after he'd tried to throw himself into the River Aire. For weeks he sat in the corner eating sandwiches and saying nothing. Slowly the story came out. He'd been a successful man with his own painting and decorating business, recently married to his second wife. One day his wife was run over and killed by joyriders. For a while before he turned up to the Crypt he had done nothing at work; he hadn't even been home. He slept rough in bin-yards. A couple had taken him in and he slept under a hole in the roof on the top floor. One day I asked him if he would decorate my stairs and hallway. He did it and charged me £30, which was nothing. Not long after I asked if he wouldn't mind looking after my house for me one weekend. I was doing catering at Christian camps and every time I went away the smack-heads burgled me. He looked after the house three separate weekends and eventually moved in as my lodger. He's been here ever since. He's back to painting and decorating. He works for City Church; he never stops and never looks back. If I ask him he tells me 'I put it down to that night I came to the Crypt'.

☐ He was an angelic faced blond lad, 18 years old. He cried and cried when he first came. He was lost; so lost. I cried with him, I put my arm round him, I wanted to love him. One day he said 'Can I talk?' He told me he felt guilty because his father had sexually abused him. He'd told his Mother but she hadn't believed him. I told him 'Jesus loves you', and just knew he was thinking 'Well where was Jesus when my Father was doing that?'. A little bit more and a little bit more he opened out and began standing up a bit straighter. He smiled a bit more. Then I didn't see him. I didn't see him for two years. One day an invitation came; he had got a job on the railways and he was getting married. I felt proud, thankful rather, that I'd played a part.

☐ A lady boarded a train from her home in Portsmouth, having bought a ticket to Leeds. When she arrived she sat on the station seats and cried hysterically until she was picked up by a caring police officer and taken to the station where she was questioned and taken to Leeds General Infirmary. The Infirmary, as always busy, took three hours to see this 38 year old lady and conclude that all she needed was somewhere to stay the night. One telephone call later and she had been shifted to the Crypt. Dianne entered the Crypt building, her face expressionless, her eyes dead. She was approached by a care worker. For some time reluctant to speak, it seemed that we would not be able to help her. Somehow the care worker eventually made a breakthrough and she agreed to come into an interview room. More silence – no response to gentle questioning. Her first words 'I've had enough of it all – I am going to kill myself, nobody cares'. Dianne wept! It was quite clear to the care worker that this situation was out of his depth. He used the silences to pray – the prayer was short 'God, help!' Sure he could try to find accommodation, but in his mind her immediate need was medical – but the hospital had turned her away.

Slowly, very slowly, the care worker started to build up some sort of relationship. Dianne clearly saw herself to be unloved, *ugly* and totally unlovable. In his experience, he had not seen anyone quite so depressed. It didn't take an expert to discern that she should be taking medicine, but she had left it all at home. She expressed how all her life she felt that she had been passed from pillar to post (and all the care worker could think of doing was passing her back to the hospital). We rang local hostels – at least, he thought, Dianne will get some rest as she hadn't slept for over 24 hours. One hostel had a vacancy but because of Dianne's state was unable to accept her – *until she had a thorough checking over by a psychiatrist*.

If Dianne was adamant about anything – it was firstly that she was not going to hospital, and secondly that she was going to end all this pain, once and for all. Somehow, some way, the first objection was overcome and Dianne allowed the care worker to take her over to the Infirmary. Several hours later she was admitted overnight into hospital until a psychiatric doctor was able to assess her. The carer prayed openly for Dianne and left her to the experts.

Two weeks later Dianne wrote a letter to the care worker: 'Thank you for your help and prayers. I think your prayers are working; I now know that God doesn't want me to end my life… and you took the time to care when I was at rock bottom. You know you did the sign of the cross on my forehead? I can still feel that cross'. This care worker is under no illusion about Dianne's future actions. She may go through the same process, perhaps somewhere else, in another town. But his confident prayer is that Jesus continues to look over her and wherever she may find herself, someone is there to remind her of her worth in God's eyes.

☐ I have been an alcoholic; no, I am an alcoholic. I've been homeless, a client at the Crypt, a resident at Faith Lodge, a volunteer there, a worker there and now I'm a Minister of an Evangelical Church. You could say that my life has seen quite a turnaround. I drank my first pint of *brown and bitter*, that's a Liverpool drink, at 17; it was what my father drank. Almost straight away I wanted to drink more than anybody else. I thought that my mates would think I was the life and soul of the party. I remember once some mates talking about drink they didn't want. 'Oh!, give it to Scouse, he'll drink anything'. And I drank it. I thought I was great because I was the only one who could do it. I didn't realise they were having a go. For over ten years I drank and drank. I held down a job, but saved nothing. Eventually after redundancy I found myself homeless. I put out my thumb to hitchhike to London. A lorry driver stopped and said he was going to Leeds. I said 'That will do'. For two nights I slept in a derelict house in Cookridge Street, before I found myself queuing outside the Crypt with other down-and-outs. It was now that I began to realise that I was running away from reality. Travelling to a derelict house to hide or drinking yourself into oblivion to escape your problems amount to much the same thing.

When you first stop drinking you count. You count the hours, then you count the days, the weeks, the months and eventually the years. I can tell you that in my case I stopped drinking 21 years ago. I know I stopped drinking when I became a Christian in 1981. Eventually the counting stops and you get on with your life. At first when I passed the back door of a pub I smelled the beer and was tempted. Now I can happily go into a nice country pub and have a lemonade.

I tell anyone who comes to Faith Lodge, whether it be a worker or client, about my past. I tell them openly. They know they can't shock me. I am a friend, an ear that will listen. Most alcoholics believe that the experts, the psychiatrists and the psychologists, don't know anything. They say to me 'I can talk to you, because you've been there'. An alcoholic will more easily tell you how much he's got left, rather than how much he's spent on drink. I've been there, done that, got the T-shirt, washed it, ironed it and thrown it away. When drink starts to cost you more than money, that's when it becomes a problem.

On a beach in Rhyl I asked Jesus to come into my life and be my Saviour. Up to that point I had been to Church just twice in my life, once to my brother's Christening and the other at the time of Winston Churchill's funeral because my Dad insisted. I found my way to Rhyl, like a lot of Liverpudlians do in the summertime. There was a children's mission on the beach; they were singing hymns and telling Bible stories. I stopped on a wall and listened. I did the same routine for three days. At the end of the third day a guy came up and said 'God's been speaking to you hasn't he?'. I thought 'We've got a right nutcase here'. He went on to say that there was a way to escape my problems. If I confessed my sins to God, I would be forgiven. I stood and argued with him for about an hour and a quarter. 'OK, I believe Jesus is the Son of God, but that was thousands of years ago'. He introduced me to his friend who was quite clever. The friend didn't give me Bible stories. He said 'I have a five year old daughter. If she was on that wall and I told her to jump, she would jump because her Father would catch her. You are sitting on a wall and your Heavenly Father is waiting to catch you'. I got down on my knees on that beach and I prayed. I was still homeless, still alcoholic, but it was the start of my turnaround.

☐ It was my very first day at St George's Crypt. I was sitting at my desk looking out of the window wondering how I was going to manage this new challenge. I looked down at the accounts in front of me when there was such a loud bang I thought someone had been shot. I jumped out of my skin, looked up and there was Andy banging on the window and shouting about the Crypt and life in general. He was drunk. I wondered what on earth it was that I had come to and whether I would be able to cope with this sort of thing every day. The next day Andy came and apologised for his behaviour.

That was Andy, drunk and verbal one day, sober and full of remorse and a lovely lad the next. Andy was the same age as me and often could be found at the door asking for me and proposing to me – when drunk!!

I remember one particular day very well. Andy turned up at the Crypt drunk as usual but not verbally abusive. I went to the door and he handed me a piece of pampas grass as a present. He said 'I would have got you a swan but I couldn't catch it'.

In my nine years at the Crypt I have learnt such a lot and mainly from those who believe they have nothing to give and nowhere to go. With the help of the Crypt they have somewhere to go and boy, do they have a lot to give.

☐ It was a happy accident really, that I should be working here. I had to give up volunteering because the smoke in the night shelter got too much for me. Tony found that I had English qualifications, so when Denise went on Maternity leave I took on secretarial work. Eventually this became a full-time post.

☐ I suppose my impression of the Charity from afar was one of extremely worthy work carried out on a shoestring. I also got the impression that the fabric of the Crypt was very much in need of modernisation.

While this was all based on nothing but surmise, I guess in some ways it was quite prophetic. Ten years on and three years into working for the Crypt I can see I was right in a number of ways. The work was done on a shoestring and the fabric was in urgent need of modernisation. Where I was wrong, however, was imagining the work was *worthy*. It was and is much more than that. It is work right at the cutting edge of human frailty – it is work which is non-judgemental and inclusive and it is, most importantly, on a daily basis living out the Christian commitment of the staff in a practical and utterly selfless manner. The Crypt is always there – it is prepared to go to places and people that many other agencies won't reach. I have worked in three charities over the last 14 years – all have their attractions but St George's has the capacity to command total commitment from the staff and volunteers. Its record of 72 years of selfless and unconditional support of people just compels you to go the extra mile.

St George's Crypt has a loyal donor base of around 3,500, many of whom have given, often sacrificially, for over 50 years. The high percentage of consistent support will be envied by many charities.

I remember one evening shortly after I started work at the Crypt in January 1999. At a reception on behalf of our 'More Than a Roof' capital appeal, the then Chief Executive of Kelda Group (Yorkshire Water) said 'There is a very sound business reason to support the work of St George's Crypt. It is much more cost effective to support this appeal as against pouring more and more money into ever more sophisticated security systems.' How right he was!

Crypt archive

For some reason the sight of
a homeless person offends people
who are rolling to their homes drunk.

When I was younger I was chairman of the Jewish Welfare Board. Like many I found the initial meetings I attended, though important, were repetitive and uninspiring. One night, after I had gone through a predictable agenda of apologies, minutes of the last meeting, financial report, two items of current business, any other business and time and date of the next meeting, I said 'Let's abandon this type of agenda and at the next meeting all return with thoughts on one word. That word will be *loneliness*'.

We had our meeting, and from it emerged mechanisms which created the first Leeds Day Centre. We quickly had 300 volunteers giving time to developing programmes that helped people. In the early stages there were few rules, though we did say that if someone took the mid-day meal then they were required to either attend a morning class or an afternoon one. We offered three or four languages, including Hebrew, sessions on crafts-skills, and did recreational things like teaching people how to play bridge. All social classes and creeds were involved and at one time throughout the week we had seventeen subjects on offer. It is a different age but I still sometimes think that we need to think afresh of ways in which we could use voluntary activities in new and interesting ways.

As a Leeds Magistrate I would often be asked to judge what we then called vagrancy cases. I never found this aspect of the work easy, for I could imagine the sheer despondency which must come upon a person who is very cold and hungry.

As the years passed, it became noticeable that at Christmas more and more vagrants appeared as the nights got colder and the feeling of loneliness increased. On one occasion I found myself sitting in judgement on an old man who was in his seventies. He had broken a window about the size of a piece of foolscap paper at the Leeds Permanent Building Society offices.

His reason was not vandalism; he just wanted to commit the small crime which would ensure that he was arrested and could sleep the night in a cell. Sitting on the Bench, knowing myself to be a Director of the damaged company, I knew that I should have declared an interest, but I decided my duty was with the man and that we could too easily afford the pane of glass. Understanding and mercy must temper justice. To my mind he needed help, not punishment. Real criminals rarely sleep the night out in places like the Crypt or the Salvation Army Hostel.

In the 1960s what we now call a football hooligan had to be arrested as 'drunk and disorderly'. In those days the maximum fine was £5 for being drunk and another £5 for being disorderly, so having determined that the youth in question got £18 per week I then looked around for what seemed to be a reasonable fine for a young single drunken man who had been wandering up and down the street intimidating people. I could tell by his attitude that he could afford to pay, but when I asked him what was his best offer he said 'Half a crown per month'. On my reckoning it would be just under seven years before the fine was paid. I said this was acceptable but made the condition that it should be paid at Gipton, the farthest police station I could think of from Elland Road, at 3.15 p.m. on a Saturday. It's said that he paid the total fine immediately.

Most vagrants I have met from the Crypt or similar places were not like that at all. It is true that many of them who were drunk lived in squalor and could be disruptive, yet for all that it was not difficult to understand their underlying sadness. I have often felt that the world divides into two types of people; those who are the leaders and those who are the led. What unites them is a loneliness often found in each group. Both require a social life and a feeling that they are being helpful and that is why, over the years, I have come to place great emphasis on the need for us all to think seriously about public service.

As soon as they know you are nobody, they straight away know that you can't go to the police.

☐ Yorkshire County Cricket Club supports St George's Crypt because we see it as an important part of our outreach work within the city. In the past we have provided bats and memorabilia for fund-raising purposes. We endeavour to be involved in other ways as well. Before a recent game between Yorkshire and the West Indies tourists, I was asked if I could arrange for Ridley Jacobs, the Test wicket keeper and a committed Christian, to visit the Crypt. Ridley agreed and asked if Jimmy Adams the Captain, and also a Christian, might come along. On the Tuesday evening, following the second day's play, I took Ridley and Jimmy to the Crypt. They talked with staff and the people they care for, played table tennis and generally made a big impression. The thought occurred to me that if that is how Christians behave, we could do with a few more in the game. Since then our Club, through the good offices of Shaun Callighan, our Catering Manager, has supplied the Crypt with substantial amounts of food, which is often available if a match finishes early. After the Test Match when England beat the West Indies in less than two days, we were left with three days' food on our hands. The West Indies weren't the only losers. Refunded tickets cost the Cricket Board nearly half a million pounds, the West Indies sponsors lost three days of prime TV publicity and the opportunity to offer important guests corporate hospitality. The winners of course were St George's Crypt. But that can't be a bad thing can it? If ever there is food to spare Shaun Callighan *tips the wink* and it goes to St George's.

☐ A lot of architecture, both modern and historical, has been about fitting people into buildings. With the St George's project we had to consider how to fit a building around people, but when I visit the Crypt now and look at the ducting in the corridor by the laundry I think 'Yuk!' It's one of the things to think about when you're designing more for the social side of a building than from an architectural perspective; or indeed if you're working for a charity with limited financial resources. It took a long time to raise the money to rejuvenate this building. The truth was it had to be done. The Crypt was under threat from both the Fire Department and the Environmental Health; they would have condemned the place to close if plans hadn't been drawn up. Once you went into the innards of the old building you couldn't find your way out. The first part of the brief had to be a ring corridor, so that whichever direction you ran in, you could escape a fire. I was one of three architects who put a presentation to the Board of Trustees. My idea was selected. The basic concept was to bring light into a place that hadn't known daylight before. Also to free the whole space up, so that it can be easily reorganised in the future. It was a slow, painstaking and labour-intensive job, with a lot of hand digging. I'm very pleased with the outcome. I wish I could have done something with the ducting!

☐ I believe I first came to the Crypt when it was dark and a bit dirty. My next occasion to visit came when David Goldspink asked me to be Patron of the 'More than a Roof' appeal. I then came to do the rededication. I felt the place had been hugely transformed and that transformation was reflected in the people there themselves. It shone and it shone, in lots of colours. And I could feel the welcome. People were not being treated as things, or even clients, but as people.

☐ The 1830s church was too warm for my liking, then it occurred to me that this was bound to be the case for the place of worship stood above the Crypt and they supplied each other with warmth. They were interdependent though not artificially so. In the old days it must have been very difficult to heat, having as its foundations vaults for the dead.

As I had approached it on this cold February night, I noticed that to the outsider there appeared to be two entrances; one in the basement and one above. I made for the bottom one, and found myself with some young people in many layers of clothing looking for a meal and a cup of something. They rang a door-bell and were let in with a friendly nod. Twenty feet above them, others were walking along the south side of the church, and I realised that I should be up there if I wanted to attend the evening Service.

The stairs are steep and although the building is on a slope, you wonder why the architect spent so much on lifting it above Great George Street. Inside it is a lofty gothic building with few embellishments. Recently it has undergone a distinctive restoration and is, I should think, in a better physical condition than it has been since the opening.

It is clear from the beginning of the service that this is a congregation that is coming to terms with the modern age. We sing a lot of hymns and songs, all in clear copyright and none dated from before 1992. These are sung with enthusiasm to key-board and guitar. In the services of my youth the clergyman came in with great ceremony. Not here. I was studying the hymn book, looked up and there he was speaking quietly, apologising for the microphone being temporarily out of action. I went back to the hymn book, looked up and he had been joined by a woman minister. If you told me that they arrived like angels I would have been prepared seriously to consider the proposition. The people in church that night were young people, the vast majority were not yet 25.

In its own way it was a beautiful service, fresh and invigorating though with not many concessions to the past although the beautiful old hymn *O Love That Will Not Let Me Go* was sung half way through the service. When the communion bread was broken it was real bread, not a ritualised wafer. Lay people assisted the clergy in administering the sacraments to the congregation. Sometime in the latter part of the service I found my mind wandering. Sometimes it was going up to the rafters but more often to the Crypt which lay beneath us. I began to think about what bound and what separated the two groups of young people and came to the conclusion that they were more similar than dissimilar. Both were coming to terms with a new age and trying to discover where they fitted in. Both groups challenged, and in their different ways were challenging.

☐ When it was confirmed that the heating system was beyond repair we felt that this might be the time to bring the building into the modern era, so we took the congregation into exile. Each Sunday for two years we trundled a caravan of liturgical gear and hymn books up the hill to St Michael's Roman Catholic College as architects and workmen remodelled the inner space of our 1838 building. The next year we encamped in the semi-derelict United Reformed Church close to the Parkinson Building of Leeds University. On Wednesday lunch times we would return, usually about a dozen of us, to take Holy Communion; we were the Church renewing itself in the building rubble of the nave of our old church.

Sometimes, as we came together, I said that we should learn to relish this time, and come to see that these months were an exhilarating time of testing, for when confronting decisions and learning to be flexible we were at our best. At one point, early on, I asked that we should choose from our congregation fifteen people who would oversee the project. As we thought things over I advanced the opinion that we should select from the gathering the most conservative people who we trusted, so that the heritage would be represented, and place them together with those who were innovators,

those who thought more about the future. It was a challenge. When I went to the first meeting I could have drawn chalk lines on the floor as to where the factions would sit. As time passed people started to talk out of role and showed what could be accomplished through trust.

All this gave us a head start when we found ourselves confronted with the need to re-fashion the Crypt. Water leaks had made us rethink the church; it was the sudden death of our colleague Don Paterson that forced us to look at the forces which shaped our sister organisation.

His death was a blow, for his personality had shaped the organisation, and in that pause for breath we looked at every option. Some argued that this might be the time to call it a day. Unlike the 1930s, there were now other agencies to take up the challenges. Others felt, having given sacrificially to help the church, it would be difficult to find that sort of money again, but others said that having done it once we could do it again. We should restructure and build on the foundations Don and his predecessors had left us. It was a risky strategy but this view prevailed.

We all recognised that our task would be made easier if we knew and described what we wanted, so we sat and drew up the mission statement in the days before the term was invented. The vision rested on the teachings of Jesus. He ministered to all people regardless of race, rank or station and so would we. We would continue to provide a sanctuary where we could work and worship with all who sought support, justice and spiritual hope.

Soon after I arrived, I took our church council a visual aid. Three hula-hoops bound to a cane with sticky-tape and made to look like magnifying glasses. The three glasses celebrate our primary task to worship God as Mary did in the Magnificat, *My Soul Magnifies the Lord*. The hoops were covered in Perspex and were overlapping. On one was the words in Letraset *Share the Gospel,* on the second *Renew the Church* and on the third *Care for Society*.

Three aims in one drawn from the manifesto in St Luke chapter four, which Jesus took for his ministry. I still have them close to my desk, and although they now look dog-eared, they are in essence mint fresh.

☐　On 14 September I rejoiced with the vast congregation when the transfigured Crypt was rededicated by the Archbishop of York for the continuance of the work into the twenty-first century. And what a transformation! Well lit, aired and warmed, designed to provide areas for community fellowship and food, with facilities for private interview and counselling and emergency night accommodation. All this backed by offices equipped for a professionally caring service which must meet high standards of competency in co-operation with the Statutory Services. *Only the best will do for God* is the philosophy which has guided the planning, fund-raising and building of the new Crypt, and now it stands ready to serve those to whom life has consistently denied the best.

This new sophisticated environment has to be suffused with the same genuine friendship and love which countered the dark atmosphere of the old Crypt. Then, it almost seemed that the very grimness of the setting drew out an excess of love, joy and laughter as if to spite the darkness and bleakness of the lives coming in for shelter. Will it, I wonder, be easier or harder to make folk feel welcome, wanted, understood and loved in the updated Crypt? At the heart of the new building is a Chapel, and there lies the answer to my wondering!

☐ Like the word *Crypt* itself, the place sounded dark, stale and eerie. The challenge was to open it up and make it more serviceable. It was one hell of a challenge. Up to that point I think it was one of the biggest jobs I'd worked on; a massive task of underpinning. During refurbishment the whole Church was held up on the steelwork stilts like a skeleton. All the internal walls had to be pulled out and sometimes because of the eccentric Victorian designs and additions we didn't know where we were going. One wall that we expected to be twelve hundred millimetres thick, turned out to be a metre. You couldn't relate a measurement to the building because of all the little rooms. It was difficult to make a method statement or compile a risk assessment. Then mysterious occurrences began to take place. Some of the lads working late at night to float off floors started to talk about lights falling down for no reason and cold draughts when there was no wind. The concrete gang reported footprints in freshly laid concrete. We told them not to be silly – 'Ghosts aren't heavy enough to leave footprints'. Even so, the reports were minuted in a site meeting. A lady Vicar came down and they broke bread and said a blessing. We were still scared. Before we managed to install full power to the whole building, everything worked off big diesel generators. If there was a late service one of the gang would have to come down and turn the generators off when they'd done. I came down one night in the pitch black with my daughter and a torch. A sudden noise didn't half make the hair stand up. One of the labourers came down one night to do the same job with two dogs. He told me later that the two dogs wouldn't go inside. You don't know about these things. It was a very interesting job though, and I'm proud of the standard of workmanship.

☐ It wasn't the people who came to the Crypt that frightened me. It was the thought of all them dead bodies behind the walls.

☐ We discovered a lot of things we didn't know much about during the refurbishment, pillars that didn't seem to support anything and a circular stone that seemed to go right down from the Church into the earth. I believe that a font may have stood on it at one time and that splashed holy water would bless the foundations.

☐ When you are the eldest of thirteen children, you quickly turn into a pleaser or everybody's mother. It's hard. I can't blame one thing for my sleeping sickness, but trying to do for everybody may have had something to do with it. I had sleeping sickness so bad I could only stay awake for a couple of hours a day. I couldn't do the housework or anything. I decided gently to go back to education. I took an O-level in English at the local college in Pudsey; in fact my daughter was starting her O-levels at school at the same time. I got an A grade the year after. Next, I wanted to do A-levels; the Doctor told me to do just one, but I did two, in Literature and Psychology. Leeds Poly had introduced a new course in Combined Studies at Honours Degree level. I did two evenings a week for seven years, but I got my degree in the end. Then I went on to do a Postgraduate teacher training certificate at Holly Bank College in Huddersfield. Over ten years of study it took me, and I'd left school at 15, over 20 years before that. I think that's why I can identify well with the sort of people for whom education doesn't come easy.

My first big teaching job was at Armley Prison, and I came to relish it. On the first day I was that frightened my tongue stuck to the top of my mouth and I had to shove a Polo in to make me talk. A big lad with lovely blue eyes came up to me and said 'Are you scared of us?' 'Should I be'?

After that the ice was broken and I went on to get a lot of valuable teaching experience. I had great support as well. There's a woman Chaplain there called Pat Jakeways; she still supports me now, she's brilliant. After the prison I worked in bail hostels and discovered I had a talent for working with the disadvantaged. I'll never forget when I applied to teach at Armley and they said 'Why should we employ you?'. I said 'Because I speak the same language as the students'.

When you stay for the night with a lot of different friends, you soon run out of friends.

I suppose I ended up at St George's because they think I speak the same language as the people who come here. It's not easy to teach here; it's a fluid population and added to that you have a number of vulnerable people who don't want it on show that they can't read or write. It might be a good thing to be out there amongst it all so people can see education taking place, but it's hard. Sometimes the basic literacy class becomes a 'help to fill in forms' class. All these forms, and at the end of the day all they want is somebody to cuddle them. A pat on the hand here and a hand on the shoulder there is just as important as showing somebody how to spell a difficult word. I once did a workshop on hugging in prison, believe it or not! Of course it all leaves you open to being hugged in the middle of Leeds when you're out shopping with your best clothes on, by somebody who has just come up out of a doorway. I've ended up having a good rapport with criminals and the homeless; I think they look on me as a mother-figure. Which brings me back to where I started, and all I ever wanted to be was a sex-symbol!

☐ The Crypt is a place with a lot of doors and I know that one of the things that we must do is to work in a wide variety of ways to make sure that they are not kept locked. We are in the business of opening doors. Then we have to make sure that the provision is secure.

When it comes to educational work I am optimistic. It is never easy to get people to day-time classes but there is something about the atmosphere here that all the teachers like and the feeling is good. We are all sure that more will come to our evening classes. At the moment we are offering art and basic skills but as the partnership with our college develops then we will build on that base. We are already giving intensive English language support to ten refugees as we respond to new wants. We are also thinking of ways in which we can link the very successful creative writing classes to the computer programming.

When you look at the premises, then you see that this is a real asset. There is a shop, a kitchen and plenty of space, but what is probably more important, there is a willingness to think about learning and training opportunities in new ways. That is worth a lot.

☐ All I know is when it comes to the time for me to pop my clogs, I've got Him to face. And when the Lord asks me what I've been doing, to give an account of my stewardship, I shall have to tell him about the night I laid in bed and started thinking 'What am I going to do with my life? It's about time I got out there and started to do something'. I still jump out of that bed at six o'clock every morning. I'm out of the house by seven, I go to St Anne's Cathedral for Mass and I'm here by half past eight to sort out clothes. There's some lovely gear. You can get a pair of jeans for thirty pence and a coat for fifty.

I've got a purpose. I'm doing it for the Lord. It's better than sitting at home and watching Richard and Judy. It was all dark passages and cubby holes when I first came, like the back o'beyond and it took a long time for me to find my way round. It wasn't as clean as it is now, but the food was good. There was a lot of rudeness and bad language, but I used to just say 'Hello' and carry on. You have to take the rough with the smooth. I always worked on the night shelter at first, but it got to be a bit daunting. I'm 86 soon and I was getting a bit frightened. There's not a soul knocking about round here at night time and I had to walk to City Square for my bus home. I had to change my tactics, so they put me on the day shift.

I'm in St Augustine's Legion of Mary so I do all sorts to help poorly folk and them in need. I might make a little report for the Priest 'Well, you see Father, you could do with going to see so and so'. I try not to judge. If I hear something about somebody, I try to imagine what they might be suffering.

I've met all sorts of people at St George's Crypt; doctors, royalty, and on a Friday when I go home I think 'Thank God I've been'.

▢ I had to go to Clarendon Road for an appointment at Black's Solicitors, and for some reason I arrived about half an hour early. I decided to walk round and get a bit of fresh air. I saw this big, dark, gaunt building. I stepped inside and was very impressed. I came to learn that St George's is absolutely unique. Both my wife and me had done the rounds; Baptist, Methodist, Roman Catholic. Most church congregations you find these days are old. And there's a full stop after that. Here they have youngsters to oldsters and all points in between, especially students from the University, and that's got to be good.

We were in Los Americas, Tenerife. Near there is a place called Los Christianos. What a culture shock we had! The pastor there, Tom Reston, welcomes you and says 'Come in and leave your denomination at the door'. There are people there from all points of the compass; north, south, east and west. Somebody asked me 'Which church do you worship at in England?' When I told them St George's they said 'Oh! We've heard of that!'

▢ Most people who come here to look around, either as volunteers or visitors, have an image problem. If they know nothing about us then they see the people who come here as a crowd of noisy, brawling, old drunks; that's not the case at all. Of course there are the good and the bad like everywhere else, but that isn't the impression those who know the place would come up with.

I have been coming here for well over six years and I am now on the staff. Over those years I have seen some physical changes but the atmosphere that I encountered when I first came through the door on a placement from college is basically the same. There were a lot of young people there then and there are a lot here now. I still see the same things, old hands helping the young ones to settle to this sort of life, giving them the benefits of their experience. Kindness can be seen in little things; I have seen an old man in his seventies giving his last fag and some bits of food to a younger one just out of prison with no other support than what was offered.

For a time things seemed less kindly. In the Thatcher years; people were taught that the people you looked after were your immediate family, then it was 'me, me, me'. Things are changing slowly, but I think that now that sort of thing has been rubbished. We are slowly getting somewhere. That said, I think that it will always be the poorer end who are the most supportive, for generally the more you have the more you want.

▢ The Crypt has touched me at various times in my life. The first time I really knew about it was when Mr Dickinson, a committed Christian who taught me at Secondary School, told me that he volunteered here. I thought then that it must be a good place, because Mr Dickinson, like a lot of teachers just after the war, was a well-rounded, sensible, well-liked man. Leeds schools then were full of teachers who had seen life and were not just fresh out of University. Strangely enough, the Crypt came back to me when I worked as a shoe repairer. People from well-heeled backgrounds would come in and say 'I'm donating these shoes to St George's, but will you put a new sole on first'. I'd repair them and then send them down. After I finished with the shoe repair business I needed to take a part-time job and what better place for me than here. I worked endless, solitary hours before, now I find I can work and talk to people.

▢ We get a lot of tinned beans sent here. When we warm up a great pan-full, we might open 58 tins. They all go in, Heinz, HP, Netto; it takes some doing opening 58 tins of beans.

▢ You open the bin bags and first sniff at it. If it smells bad or is maggoty, like sometimes happens, you don't bother investigating. Next step, you look and think 'Is it worth it; will these things sell?'. Some people have the mistaken idea that if someone is homeless or in bed and breakfast accommodation they'll be grateful for anything. It doesn't work like that. You don't want a pair of pants down to your knees, or an old suit. You want something fashionable.

The stuff we know that we can sell is put ready for the shop; the other stuff is re-bagged for recycling. Some of the stuff comes already folded and pressed. Our only decision then is 'Is it fashionable?' One day, six Romanians who had fled in fear of their lives in the clothes they stood up in arrived. One man had the sole hanging off his shoe. They had no English, but with a series of gestures and smiles we were able to kit them out. It was a very satisfying moment to watch them admiring their new outfits. They were all terribly pleased, especially the man with his sole hanging off.

☐ St George's has always looked forward and been inclusive. At one time we had services in Lithuanian and Latvian. If we don't continue to look out we will look back. We must continue to meet at the point of need.

☐ Life in our complex society is difficult for anyone on a low income. But think how much more difficult it must be if your English is limited too. The Crypt, in co-operation with Leeds' Park Lane College, provides a base for language lessons for asylum seekers and other potential immigrants. These English sessions, led by Hilda Polley and Haydn Tomlinson, concentrate on everyday language. Here are a few examples of students' first experiments in getting some words from their strange new world down onto paper:

Above:
Part of our Womens Work –
visiting homes of needy families
1951

From Dokmai Peek
(Thailand)

Thai food temples
Happy people
Ancient buildings
Islands
Loikranthong
Ayuthaya
Nature
Dancing

From Sara Yacob
(Spain)

Sara is **S**panish
Sarah speaks **A**rabic
Sarah likes **R**ice
Sarah loves **A**pples

From Tamara Cojocaru (Moldova)

My son Roman
Romanian
Six years **O**ld
eats **M**eat
Apples
Nice and naughty

☐ I didn't speak English when I first came and didn't have a car, but I had a job in the catering canteen at LGI. I came on the bus and then walked down. At quarter past seven in the morning I saw half-drunk, half asleep people walking near the Crypt. Sometimes they would wave a bottle or try to talk to me. 'Who are these people?' I wondered. Some of the other cleaners told me 'They're tramps'. I would ask 'What does that mean?' If somebody had told me then, that 25 years later I would be working here, I wouldn't have believed it.

Life went by. I got a good job in the hard world of advertising. But my relationship was falling apart. I had great guilt around the issue of divorce. I wanted to be right with God, and my upbringing and the values I had been taught by the Roman Catholic Church back in Warsaw made me want to search for some answers.

A massive marquee was put up by Christians in Birstall. I was on my way to keep-fit one evening and as I passed the big tent a voice in my head said 'Margaret, you look after your body, what about your soul?' I just knew I had to go into that marquee. I had never heard the term 'born again', but even that night, some of the guilt I had been struggling with started to loosen its grip. When you are little you set out on a pattern of prayer; you learn to do it parrot fashion. I had parroted prayers all my life. Suddenly my prayers became conversations. I started to like myself; I felt like a blossom. Instead of 'Me, Me, Me', I showed interest in other people and their problems. Previously if I'd had a toothache I wouldn't hear of anything else, because this was my important toothache.

I was attracted towards counselling and took courses. 'Yes, this is for me' I thought. I volunteered to work at the Crypt on Monday evenings. I wouldn't miss my Monday evenings here for anything. I still had my good job in advertising; I gave audio-visual presentations during the day and gave out soup and bread in the evening. Then I applied to do paid work here. I took a big drop in salary, but that's what I wanted to do.

Sometimes clients here come straight into my face. They swear and shout but I won't move. I know that they're not lashing out at me personally, they're expressing anger. And I no longer ask 'Who are these people?'.

☐ The inspiration of all the outreach and social service at St George's came from the Gospel message of love, and the uplifting worship in the vast church built on the foundation of the long narrow tunnels of the old Crypt. Don Robins believed that in the sordid surroundings of a busy city, with its appalling slum areas, people needed a place of beauty, and an experience of beauty in worship. The church, open daily, with its soft lighting and its floral decorations, was an oasis for any who called to pray, or simply to sit and think. The Sunday services led by a fine organ and full choir, with preaching challenging the congregation to live out the second commandment 'to love your neighbour', provided the call and the courage upon which the Crypt depended for generosity in the constant sacrifice of time and money.

☐ The 'A' Team, Princess Anne, the Lord-Lieutenant, the Rector and a Lady-in-Waiting went with the Director and I was put in charge of the 'B' Team. It was a complicated job. I had to make sure that the leader of the City Council, the Lord Mayor, the High Sheriff and a much larger party did not catch up with the Princess Royal, then towards the end we were required to overtake so that they could all be lined up to shake the royal hand. To do this I had to act decisively but with understanding. That day things went well and all got a photograph of themselves in conversation with Her Highness, except me. That elusive picture was always just disappearing around the next corner. Like Brian Hanrahan in reverse, 'I counted them all in and then I counted them all out'. That's how I like it though, working behind the scenes. The measure of my success comes in not being noticed and in making sure that we deliver a professional service based on love and compassion. Change has had to be managed and I hope that we have managed it, yet have been careful to see a variety of points of view. There is a rich ecumenical dimension to the staff and this is reflected in the glorious array of worship styles and theology seen. Sharing in this way gives us all great support and when the doors are open we are a team and a very efficient one too.

Left:
Evening meal being served
1951

Crypt archive

Our day-to-day work varies. Sometimes we are thinking well ahead and looking to see how we can introduce education courses which can receive accreditation, and in that way answer the need to help send some of our clients into formal education. On other occasions I am suggesting that it is not helpful to distribute the Christmas mince-pies in their aluminium holders for we are trying to limit the use of drugs, not hand on some of the required equipment. Asylum seekers requiring one-to-one help with language skills and staff needing training seminars on drugs and a hundred other things, sometime or other need to be considered by the team. In total about 40 people are paid workers here or in the church. This is a significant work place.

I see the Crypt in the great tradition of the medieval, monastic church, and although a Methodist, I take strength from that ethos. The great monasteries at their best provided for the needy by balancing the Christian ethos with a professional practice. They didn't have to cope with Health and Safety regulations or heroin like we do. Otherwise, little separates their work from ours.

Something of that heritage is found in a service we have every Thursday night; it is based on the order of service understood now as it was seven centuries ago. Readers of who-dunnits or watchers of television will know that the detective Cadfael often breaks off from his investigation of a murder to attend Compline. When the day reaches its end those of us who are still here gather in meditation and prayer; the anchorage is that ancient Order of Service. Strength is given and our lives renewed.

☐ It was me who mentioned a food hygiene course in the first place. I started my course last September and I'll be doing my exams soon. I wanted to get my food hygiene certificate, so that when I go to a Job Centre I've a better chance of getting a job in a kitchen. But the main reason is to prove my social worker was wrong. They took my little boy off me because they said 'You can't do anything right for him'. I'll admit I didn't read to him, but that was because I was ashamed in case I got it wrong. I've got all the Disney books, but I just used to read them to myself. I've had to read a book properly for the first time to do this course, and I've watched a half-hour video. I think I'll get my certificate. My son is also doing well. He passed his seven-year-old maths test and his English. I'm allowed to see him every six weeks. I'd like to work at Asda. I do my shopping there and the staff seem nice.

☐ Ron Bent and Albert Palmer were great, although Ron got a bit aggressive when he was frustrated. They would sit in the front pews and Ron would say 'Look Albert! That's our Don up there'. If anybody important came to the service, they followed them down the aisle like a couple of choirboys. When Ron got his flat he invited Margaret Thatcher for tea. She didn't respond. At my wedding I decided I didn't want everybody to sit through endless telegram messages, so we picked two to read out. One was from the Archbishop of Canterbury, the other was from Albert Palmer.

☐ A lot of business people and successful people for that matter live sheltered lives. A Professor at Leeds University said to me years ago 'Where else would I get to have a conversation with a dustbin man? I can do it here when we're both volunteering to wash up'.

☐ I could preach the sermon of the Good Samaritan or the Prodigal Son and know that we were not just shooting a line. This was no paradiddle; downstairs people were rolling their sleeves up and getting on with it. On the one hand we were validating a theory and on the other, developing a fellowship between volunteers, business people and clients.

☐ I never got to the point where I was sitting on a wall in the wind and rain drinking methylated spirits, but I was certainly on that road. You see, you deceive yourself at first, then you start deceiving others, until the only important thing in your life is the next drink. I was stationed in Germany attached to the Signals Regiment. A double brandy with coke cost less than a Mark and we were getting 10 Marks to the pound. I was in the Officers' Mess on my own, the place hadn't been tidied up. There were dregs left in a lot of the glasses. I put all the dregs into one glass and drank it. You realise later that you are reaching the depths of your addiction when alcohol is so cheap and you are drinking a cocktail of other people's left-over drinks.

☐ He turned up at the Crypt door with the map of Britain in scars on his forehead. One step forward, three to the side and a bottle in his hand for balance. Every time I saw him he had a smile on his face and fresh cuts on his head. Even the paramedics knew him by his nickname. A space became available at Regent Terrace. Regent Terrace is a *damp* house, meaning they are allowed to drink in the garden. He still takes to the drink, but when I bob by from time to time I know he's cared for and loved.

☐ Every time I do go back, more of the people I grew up with have gone to Arkansas or Maine. I don't like to come back any more. If you spoke the Gaelic in Spiddeal your parents got £200 per year. I learned the Gaelic. Now it's like Latin; a dying language. I was educated by the Christian Brothers; they'd hit you across the head with a leather, but they were gentlemen. They were great believers in sport; hurling, Gaelic football – if you dribbled the ball they'd clip you round the ear, 'We don't play that foreign game in the Gaelic fields'. And if you queued up in the morning without a handkerchief in your pocket you'd have a rap across the knuckles. When I came to England I was like a proper gentleman of the road. I toured all over with a friend of mine, a day's work here and a day's work there, skippering some nights, in the local spike the next, and on a pew at the back of a church on another. You could do that then. Now there's not a lot of work about, the spikes are called Reception Centres and the churches get locked because of vandalism.

☐ I was never violent. I worked my fingers to blisters. I had a family life and took the kids on trips every weekend when I wasn't working. We went to Pontefract Races, Doncaster, Thirsk – all over. When my wife left me to go and live in Hull I didn't know what to do. One day I was waiting at the Pontefract bus stop when I broke down. Nobody helped me. The trouble with Leeds is this; there's a lot of money here, but it's going to them that have got it already, and when you want their attention they always seem to be looking the other way.

☐ On Friday nights they let me sleep here; it keeps me out of the cold for one more night. I come back about half past eleven at night for tea and biscuits and then they put mattresses down for about ten of us. At half past seven they get you up. A hot shower and a ten pence Bic razor can be very uplifting when you live on the streets. I'm on the *Dihydrocodeine* treatment at Springfield Mount at the moment. It brings you slowly off the heroin. When I was at the boarding school in Norfolk I played the English horn and did a bit of acting. Performance is something that I would like to go back to if it's not too late.

☐ I have a routine every day and do my washing on a Sunday. I don't want to be lonely in my house. Today, for instance, I went to Mind Day Centre in Dewsbury for tea, biscuits and a bit of a chat. I came to Leeds in the afternoon and I always call at the Crypt for a bit of soup and bread before I go home. It's only an hour on the bus back to Heckmondwike. Did you know that the poet William Wordsworth wrote about my home town:

> 'This is a book I do not like,
> Send it back to Heckmondwike'.

He turned up at the Crypt
door with the map of Britain
in scars on his forehead.

☐   Whether you have strayed far off like the prodigal,
or come to yourself and realised 'What a bloody fool
I've been', you can be sure of one thing; when you
come to that Crypt door you will be welcomed and not
judged straight away. The hospitality at the Crypt is
a part of the history of the Christian tradition. A part of
the Sikh tradition come to that. Go to the Sikh Temple
and you will be given food. When Jesus said 'Whatever
you do for the least of my people, you do for me', this
is what he was talking about. He also said 'I came that
they may have life; life in all its abundance', in order
that everybody may grow into a beautiful person.
The problem comes when people think you can wave
a magic wand over a problem and it is solved
overnight.

☐   I remember Raymond Turvey saying at one of the
openings 'Don't make it too posh'. I think he meant
leave room for the real dossers – the park bench men.

☐   I once sat down and started to write things about
my life and what I've seen others go through. It upset
me, but I did it. When I'd done I dug a hole and buried
it. One day when I'm gone somebody will dig it up
won't they? And then they'll see.

☐   When you've been a youth worker and a barmaid
and I've been both, you learn to cope. I always say that
I've got my own family, my Church family and of course
the Crypt family. I like to put my arms round these
people. I don't care if they smell or they've got lice.
I love 'em. I've had some great laughs here, and
a couple of marriage proposals. One lad nearly half my
age asked me and I told him I could never kiss a man
with his tongue pierced. Another said 'Why won't you
marry me?'. I said I didn't know. He said 'I know, it's
because you're a Christian and I'm a pisshead!'. I said
'Aye, that'll do'. My kids kid me that they won't go to
town with me any more. They say 'The only people
who talk to you are policemen and bums'.

Crypt archive

I used to give the bread out. I think we allowed three slices. A lot would ask for crusts, because there's more bread on a crust.

☐ People have spoken to me of the new Crypt as the fulfilment of my father's vision. In one way this cannot be true – in another way it is. There is no way, 70 years ago, as Don and Joe stepped into that cat-ridden tomb, that he could have envisioned what the Crypt has now become with its fabulous facilities to meet changed client needs. And yet his vision, in his preaching and in his personal action with his overalls and barrow of rubbish clearing out the Crypt – his vision was always of a Church consumed by the love of God – a love which overflowed in practical care for the marginalised and the victims of a hard and often uncaring world. That vision is fulfilled in the continually evolving ministry of St George's Crypt. 'Faith without works is dead' said St James. St George's is the evidence of faith expressed through works.

As a son of the founder of St George's Crypt, I gladly pay tribute to all those who since my father's death in 1948 have kept his vision growing – making the twin buildings of Church and Crypt an embodiment of Divine Love.

☐ It's not just a place where I'm doing my attachment from Theology College, it's a place where I've met some wonderful people; people who have taught me so many things, people with potential waiting to be recognised. When someone asks you 'How was your weekend?' you can't see them as a client and you a student. I can talk to friends about 'Justification by faith' or 'John's Gospel as a Gnostic script'. But that language is just fluff and words. I understand it and know it, not in a spiritual way, but a theological intellectual way. When I talk to clients I get more than that. They are telling their own perspective; their own life. The week before the UCAS forms were due in I changed my mind. I stopped wanting to study English and signed up to Theology at Trinity and All Saints College. The stereotypical Christian was there of course; cardigans, corduroy trousers and always strumming the guitar. Then I discovered the Crypt. I don't think I realised before what Christianity could be; dealing with people and problems. It's difficult to explain; it's something that goes on in your head. Not a week goes by here when things aren't active. A hand up here, moving closer to a destiny there. I have applied to become a volunteer when my attachment is finished. The Crypt has made such an impact on me, I can't let it go yet.